AF386545

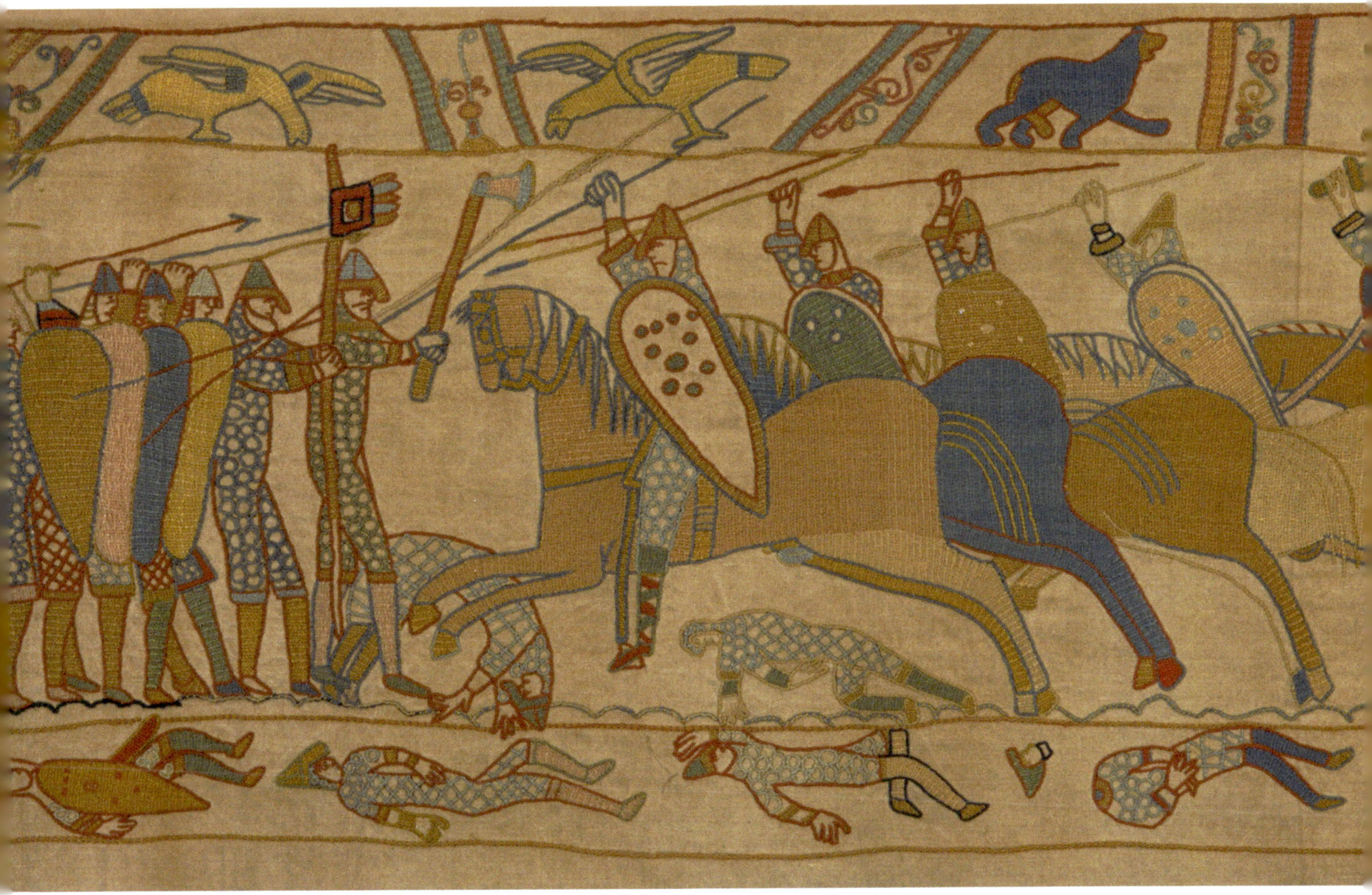

Also published by Two Rivers Press

Reading Abbey and the Abbey Quarter by Peter Durrant and John Painter
A Coming of Age: Celebrating 18 Years of Botanical Painting by the Eden Project Florilegium Society by Ros Franklin
Reading: The Place of the People of the Red One by Duncan Mackay
A Wild Plant Year: History, Folklore and Uses of Britain's Flora by Christina Hart-Davies
Silchester: Life on the Dig by Jenny Halstead & Michael Fulford
The Writing on the Wall by Peter Kruschwitz
Caught on Camera: Reading in the 70s by Terry Allsop
Plant Portraits by Post: Post & Go British Flora by Julia Trickey
Allen W. Seaby: Art and Nature by Martin Andrews & Robert Gillmor
Reading Detectives by Kerry Renshaw
Fox Talbot & the Reading Establishment by Martin Andrews
All Change at Reading by Adam Sowan
Cover Birds by Robert Gillmor
An Artist's Year in the Harris Garden by Jenny Halstead
Caversham Court Gardens: A Heritage Guide by Friends of Caversham Court Gardens
Birds, Blocks & Stamps: Post & Go Birds of Britain by Robert Gillmor
Down by the River: The Thames and Kennet in Reading by Gillian Clark

Reading's Bayeux Tapestry

READING MUSEUM

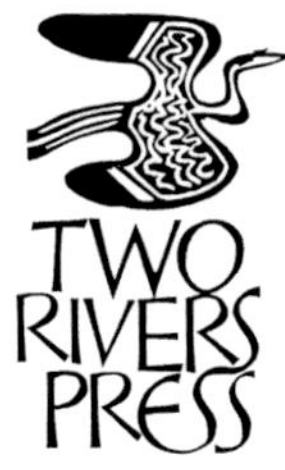
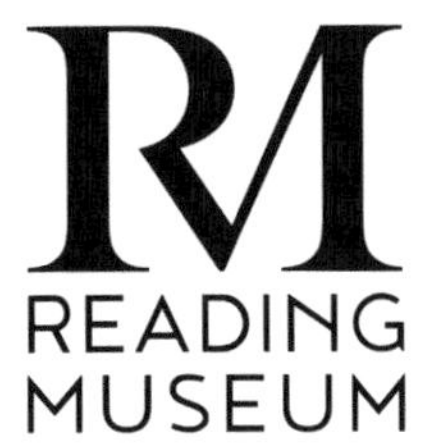

First published in the UK in 2018 by Two Rivers Press
7 Denmark Road, Reading RG1 5PA
www.tworiverspress.com

ISBN 978-1-909747-37-1

4 5 6 7 8 9

Two Rivers Press is represented in the UK by Inpress Ltd
and distributed by BookSource, Glasgow.

Cover design by Nadja Robinson with an illustration from Reading's Bayeux Tapestry
Text design by Nadja Robinson and typeset in Parisine

Printed and bound in Great Britain by Halstan & Co., Amersham

Illustrations

The picture of Elizabeth Wardle on p. 4 is reproduced with permission.
© Staffordshire County Libraries.

The picture of Arthur Hill on p. 8 is from a document owned by
The Royal Berkshire Archives (D/EX1638/71) and reproduced with
their permission. © Royal Berkshire Archives.

The picture of the Abbey ruins on p. 62 was taken by Jess Freeland
and reproduced with her permission. © Jess Freeland 2018.

All the other illustrations, including those of the tapestry itself,
are © Reading Borough Council (Reading Museum).

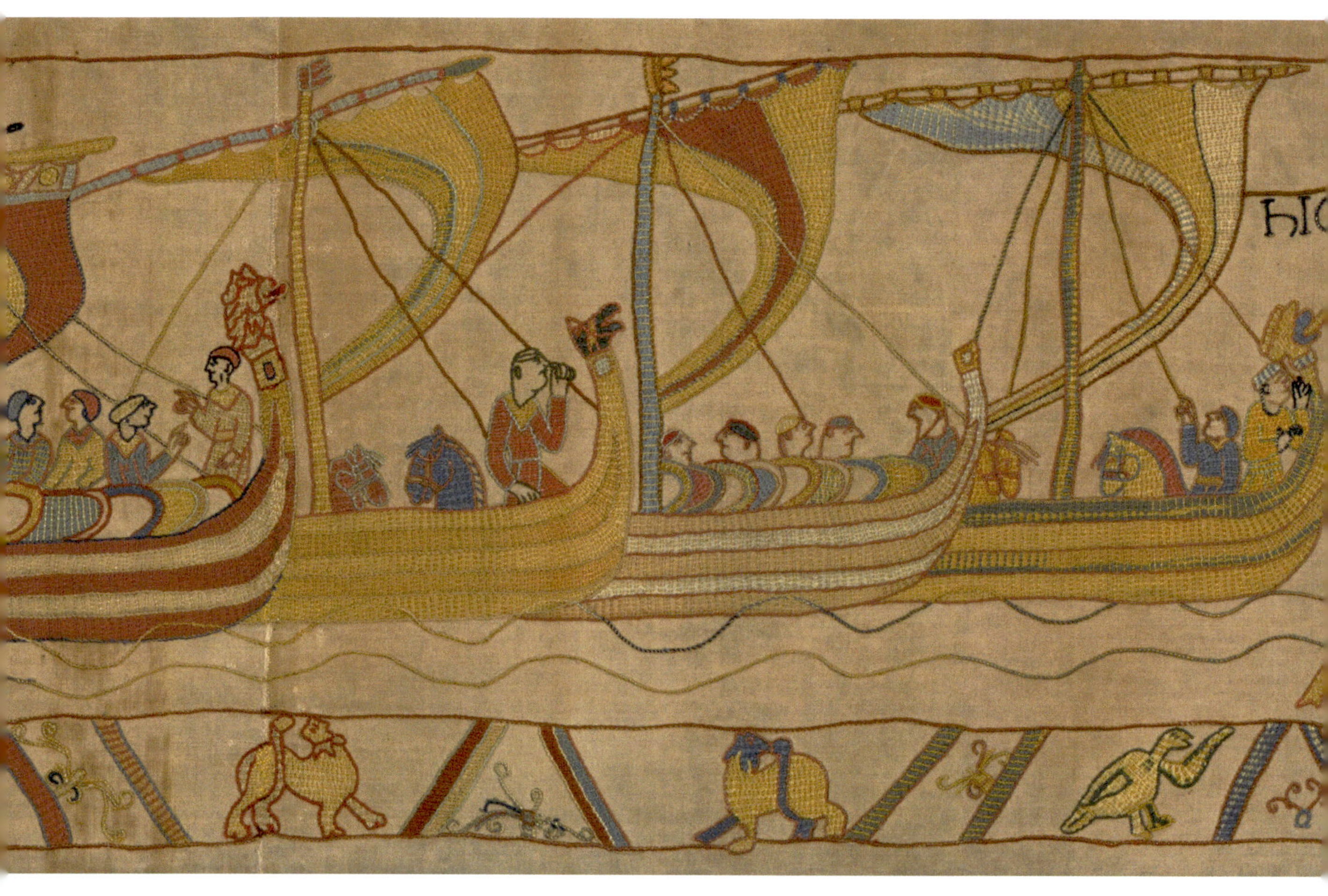
HIC

Contents

Reading's Bayeux Tapestry

The original

The original Bayeux Tapestry is on display in Bayeux Museum, Normandy. It tells a story, in pictures, of William the Conqueror's invasion of England and eventual succession to the throne having killed Harold Godwinson, the last Anglo-Saxon king of England. William established the line of Norman and Plantagenet kings.

No one knows who made the original tapestry, although specialists think it was commissioned by Bishop Odo of Bayeux (William the Conqueror's half-brother), who appears several times in it, and that it was probably made by English (Saxon) nuns in Canterbury in the 1070s. All stories have a bias, depending on the agenda of the storyteller, and the tapestry is no different. It is generally considered to be a piece of propaganda, favouring the Norman side of the story of the battle for the English throne, but a recent book, *1066: The Hidden History of the Bayeux Tapestry*, argues that it may in fact be a veiled account of the English point of view, commissioned by the French Count Eustace II of Boulogne. The secrets of this artistic masterpiece are unlikely ever to be completely revealed but the layers of meaning it contains will continue to fascinate historians for years to come.

> 'It was designed to tell a story to a largely illiterate public;
> it is like a strip cartoon, racy, emphatic, colourful, with a good deal
> of blood and thunder and some ribaldry.'
> — George Wingfield Digby, 1957

So why did a French duke, William of Normandy, have a credible claim to be the king of England?

Edward the Confessor, the last king of the 'House of Wessex', died childless on 6 January 1066 leaving a number of contenders for the throne of England. It is generally accepted that he appointed Harold, his wife's brother, as his successor, naming him such on his deathbed on 5 January. But there is also a line of evidence pointing to the fact that years earlier, he had promised

Harold, touching two reliquaries, swears fealty to William.

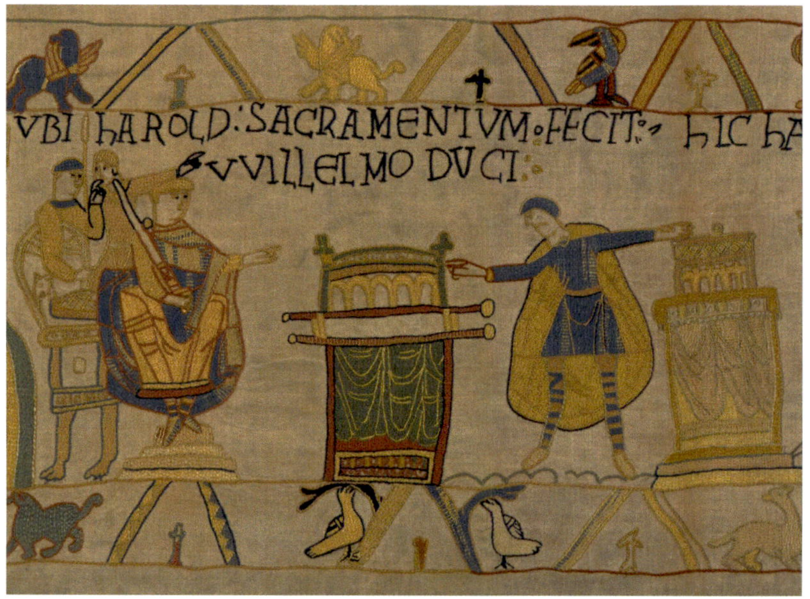

the throne to William, Duke of Normandy, the son of his cousin (related via Edward's mother, Emma of Normandy). The contemporaneous Norman historian, William of Poitiers (chaplain to William the Conqueror), wrote in his account of the invasion that shortly before the Battle of Hastings Harold had admitted that Edward had promised the throne to William, but argued that the King's deathbed promise over-rode the previous agreement.

The story in the tapestry supposedly opens with Edward sending Harold to Normandy to tell William that he will succeed to the throne of England. Harold's trip is eventful and he finds himself fighting the Duke of Brittany alongside William. A successful series of battles results in William expanding his territory and knighting Harold, who swears fealty to the Norman duke before returning to England. Soon after, King Edward dies and the next scene shows Harold betraying William's trust and breaking his oath of loyalty by accepting the Anglo-Saxon crown. What an apt opening to the story of the Battle of Hastings if you want to convince your subjects that you are, indeed, the rightful king of England!

While evidence suggests that the tapestry was made soon after the battle it depicts, propaganda is contentious, and it was perhaps too dangerous to display it publicly in such divided times. It is described, with a great deal of poetic license but with sufficient detail to indicate he had seen it, by a Norman poet, Baudry of Bourgueil, in 1102. It must have passed into the ownership of the kings of France and the only clues that exist as to its whereabouts for hundreds of years are records in the royal accounts (in Paris) of the cost of its repair in 1396 and descriptions that seem to refer to the tapestry in inventories made in 1422 and the 1430s. It must have been returned to Normandy after that, turning up in the cathedral treasury in Bayeux in 1476 with the last scene – presumably William being crowned King – missing. It was described in the treasury records as 'a very long and narrow hanging on which are embroidered figures and inscriptions comprising a representation of the Conquest of England'.

Although it is called a tapestry, it is actually an embroidery – tapestries are woven. The 70-metre/224-foot-long Bayeux Tapestry is made of linen stitched with wool threads. There are also other replicas in addition to Reading's. A New Zealand artist, Michael Linton, made a 210-foot-long replica in painted steel mosaic comprising three million tiny pieces of steel, which he finished in 2012 having taken 33 years to complete. A Norfolk-based wood carver, Jason Welch, made a 125-foot replica on 25 carved and painted wooden panels, completed in 2014. There are at least two more stitched versions residing in Canada and Denmark, completed in 1996 and 2014 respectively.

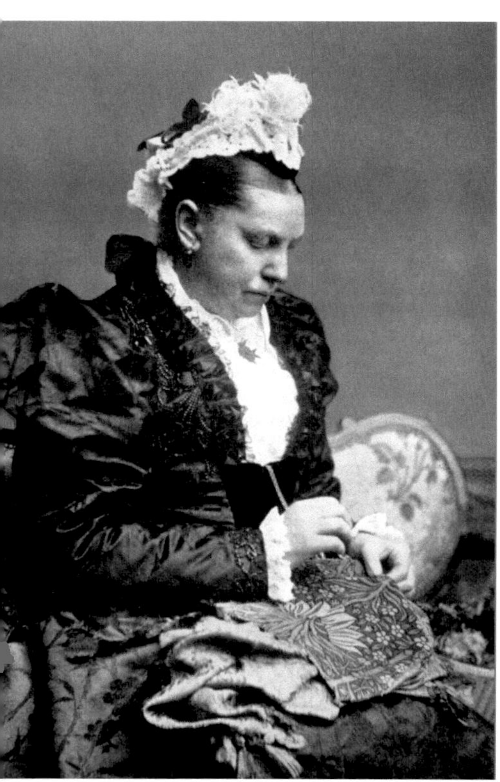

Elizabeth Wardle (1834–1902)

Reading's replica

Reading's replica of the Bayeux Tapestry is much older than these and important in its own right as a magnificent example of Arts-and-Crafts-inspired workmanship. Elizabeth and Thomas Wardle, of Leek in Staffordshire, saw the embroidery on a visit to Bayeux in 1885. They were friends of William Morris and shared his interest in the revival of ancient craft skills and the use of natural materials. They also knew Sir Philip Cunliffe-Owen, Director of the South Kensington Museum (now the V&A) where there was (and still is) a full set of hand-coloured photographs, taken in 1871, of the Bayeux Tapestry. It was after seeing these that Elizabeth developed the idea that she and her friends should make a full-size replica 'so that England should have a copy of its own'.

Elizabeth Wardle (1834–1902) was an accomplished embroiderer and had founded the Leek Embroidery Society in 1879. Her husband, Sir Thomas Wardle (1831–1909) was a wealthy and successful silk dyer and printer and promoter of the silk industry, the products of which were sold in his Bond Street shop.

Following their visit to Bayeux, work started in earnest. Thomas Wardle produced the woollen yarns, dyed to match the originals. The photographs were traced and the designs transferred to lengths of linen. The project became not only an ambitious piece of needlework but also a splendid organisational achievement. At least 35 different embroiderers were involved, possibly more, as the existence of duplicate panels suggests that Elizabeth commissioned more than one copy of particularly tricky sections and selected the best. The majority of the embroiderers were members of the Leek Embroidery Society, but not all of them lived in Leek; there were some in Derbyshire, one in Birmingham, two in Macclesfield and two in London. The impressive project was completed in just over a year and the separate sections joined together. It is a valuable indication of how short a time the original could have taken to complete.

Reading's replica is very accurate. As does the original tapestry, it depicts 626 human figures – only 3 of which are women – 190 horses, 35 dogs, 506 other birds and animals, 33 buildings, 37 ships and 37 trees or groups of trees, with 57 Latin inscriptions. There were, however, some minor adjustments

The embroiderers

Miss Alice Allen
Miss Emily A. Bate
Miss Emma Bentley (Leek)
Miss Mary Bishop
Miss Ann Cartwright
Miss Mabel Challinor
Miss Ann Clowes
Miss Elizabeth Eaton
   (Etwall, Derbyshire)
Miss Elizabeth Frost (Derby)
Miss Mary Alice Garside
Miss Patience E. Gater
Miss M.H. Gillett (Duffield, Derby)
Mrs Mary Adeline (Charles) Gwynne

Miss Elizabeth Haynes
Miss Sarah Iliffe
   (Edgbaston, Birmingham)
Miss Beatrice Lavington
Mrs Anne Mills Lowe
Mrs Elizabeth V. Lunn (Derby)
Miss Lizzie Mackenzie
   (Cheadle, Staffs)
Miss Emily Parker
Miss Alice Pattinson (Macclesfield)
Miss Florence Pattinson
   (Macclesfield)
Miss Florence M. Pearson
   (Putney, London)

Miss Margaret J. Ritchie
Miss Anne Smith (Endon Bank)
Mrs Jennie (Charles) Smith
Miss Mary E. Turnock
Miss Edith Wardle
Mrs Elizabeth Wardle
Miss Ellinor Wardle
Miss Margaret W. Wardle
Miss Phoebe Wardle
   (Cheddleton Heath)
Mrs Margaret E. Watson
Mrs Mary Edith Watson
Mrs Margaret Maude Worthington

A panel at the end of the tapestry giving details of its makers, signed by Elizabeth Wardle.

Lizzie Allen (Mrs Coombe) prepared all the drawings, which were based on hand-coloured photographs lent by the South Kensington Museum. Mrs Clara Bill joined all the sections together.

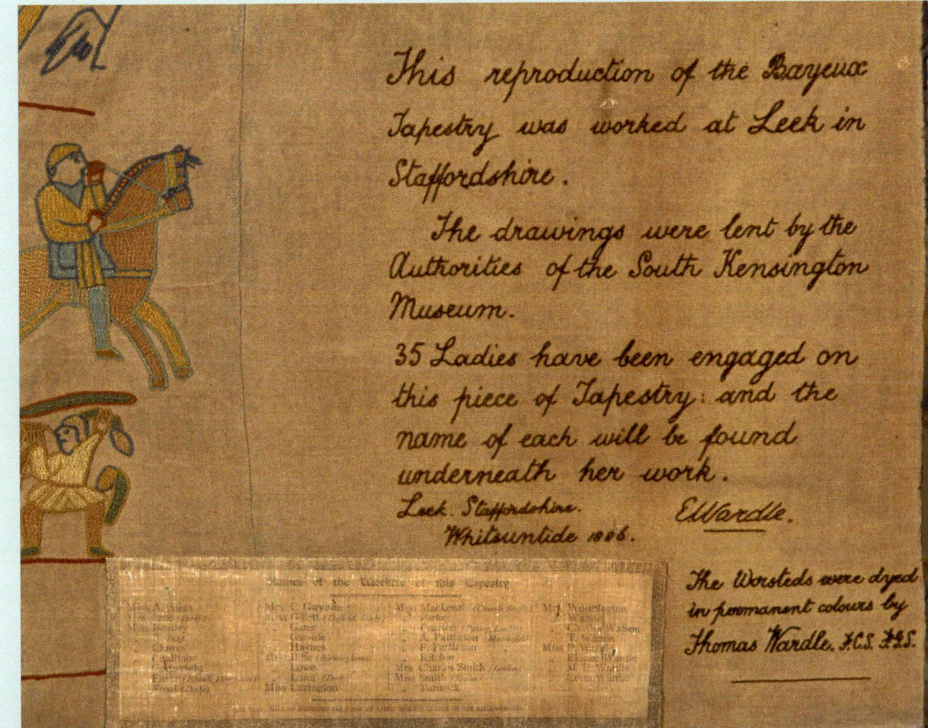

made, not, as is popularly believed, by the Victorian ladies of the Leek Society, but by the men who hand-coloured the original photographs at the South Kensington Museum. A naked figure in the borders of the tapestry was given pants, and a couple of men and some horses had their genitalia diminished or removed altogether! The replica tapestry is the same length as the original but slightly wider, as each embroiderer signed her name on a blue linen strip beneath the panel she had made. It was first exhibited in the Nicholson Institute in Leek in June 1886.

Like the original, the replica is sewn in two-ply wool yarn on linen. The main stitches are stem-stitch (for outlines and lettering) and laid-and-couched work (for filling in main areas of colour). The original colours were carefully matched by Thomas Wardle when dyeing the 100 pounds of yarn required. Natural dyes recreated the five main colours (terracotta red, blue green, sage green, buff, greyish blue). The replica has sustained some differential fading from its early display, though most sections remain bright and fresh.

Elizabeth Wardle's guide to the tapestry, published in 1887, is an abridged version of the work of the Rev. John Collingwood Bruce, who in 1856 published *The Bayeux Tapestry Elucidated*. In her guide, Wardle quotes Bruce:

'The pen of the writer of romance is not the only implement
 which confers immortality upon man. The chisel of the sculptor,
 the pencil of the painter, and the needle of the high-born dame can
 confer a lasting renown upon those whose deeds are worthy
 of being remembered.'

Why is it *Reading*'s replica?

The Leek tapestry was purchased for Reading by Alderman Arthur Hill, a former mayor and a great benefactor to his adopted town (he also bequeathed Hill's Meadow by the Thames and the former swimming baths at Cemetery Junction were named after him).

Arthur Hill was a generous friend. In 1883 – the first year of his mayoralty – when property at the rear of the Town Hall was in danger of a private sale that would prevent future extensions, Hill promptly purchased it for the sum of £2,100 and held it at the disposal of the corporation – an action for which the present generation have good cause to be thankful. He was also largely instrumental in the introduction of early closing of shops and banks in the borough, and, during each of the four years of his mayoralty, he provided at his own expense open-air band concerts in the Forbury Gardens and free Saturday evening concerts in the Large Town Hall (now the Concert Hall).

On completion of the tapestry, Elizabeth Wardle quickly arranged for it to be exhibited and it was first placed on show at the Nicholson Institute in Leek. Admission was one shilling; a season ticket was two shillings and a family season ticket four shillings. Just over 1,200 people saw it and £10 was raised. The Embroidery Society formed itself into a company to take its work on a national tour to share it with as wide an audience as possible, as well as to recoup some of their own expenditure.

The replica went to Tewkesbury, Newcastle-upon-Tyne, Stoke-on-Trent, Worcester, Chester, the United States and Germany, all during 1886. For six months in 1887 it was a major feature at the Royal Yorkshire Jubilee Exhibition at Saltaire. In 1888 it was in the Royal Pavilion at Brighton, in Blackpool in 1889, Nottingham and Derby in 1890. In 1893, shown at the National Workmen's Exhibition in London, it was awarded a Gold Medal.

The tapestry was a major success wherever it went, though it brought little financial reward for the Embroidery Society. In Brighton it actually made a loss. By 1895, when it was booked to appear in Reading, the shareholders were considering its sale. It was shown in the Town Hall in June, described as 'being on loan with the possibility of purchase'.

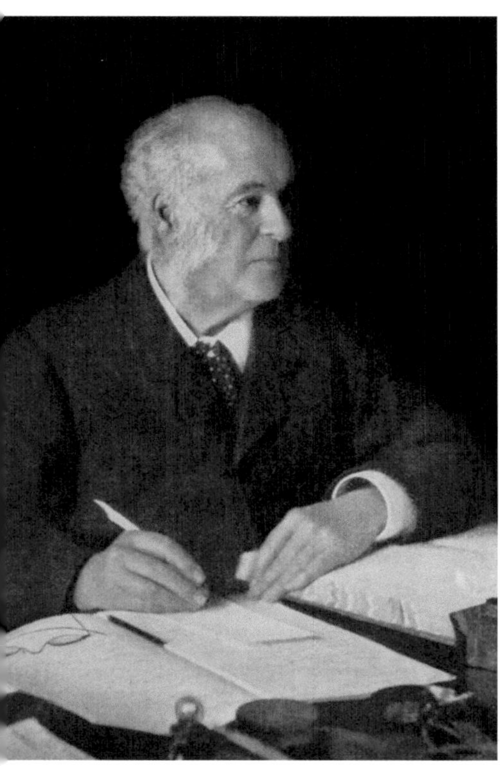

Alderman Arthur Hill (1829–1909)

In July 1895, Arthur Hill wrote to the new mayor of Reading when the Leek tapestry had been on show for a few days, offering to buy it for the town. Alderman Hill was the half-brother of Octavia Hill, the well-known philanthropist, co-founder of the National Trust and acquaintance of William Morris, so he appreciated its importance as an example of Arts-and-Crafts workmanship. The minutes of the Reading Town Council record his offer, which was accepted with gratitude. Hill offered £300 for the tapestry, together with the supports and a batch of guide books. The Embroidery Society took a vote amongst its members and the sale was agreed. Elizabeth Wardle was both surprised and disappointed; she 'never thought we should allow such a treasured possession to be sold and leave Leek'. There are suggestions, though no documentary proof, that the replica was in fact offered to Leek, but was declined.

> 'If you ... share with me the view that this work, as absolutely unique
> in its character and historical interest, would be an acquisition of
> permanent value to our new Art Gallery and the privilege of possess-
> ing it should belong to Reading, I offer the Tapestry ... as a gift to
> the Borough.'
> — Arthur Hill, Minutes of [Reading] Council meeting

Shortly after its purchase, Arthur Hill was commanded to take the tapestry to Windsor to show to Queen Victoria. Back in Reading, it was hung high up on the walls of the Small Town Hall (now the Victoria Hall) and subsequently in the Art Gallery, opened in 1897. Here, in the days before the damaging effects of light were fully recognised, it remained for nearly 30 years.

A visit by the Wardles' daughter Margaret to see the tapestry in 1927 coincided with the presence of a new director at the museum, William Smallcombe. It was clear that the tapestry needed better treatment and it was taken down, cleaned, repaired and remounted as 25 separate panels housed in dust-proof cases by Heelas of Reading.

Once again portable, the tapestry recommenced its travels. It toured again through England, including a showing back in Leek. In 1931 it went on an extensive tour of South Africa. The mid 1950s saw another sequence of exhibitions throughout England under the auspices of the Art Exhibitions Bureau. In 1965 it was once again cleaned, to prepare it for the anniversary in 1966 when it was on display at Battle Abbey overlooking the site of the

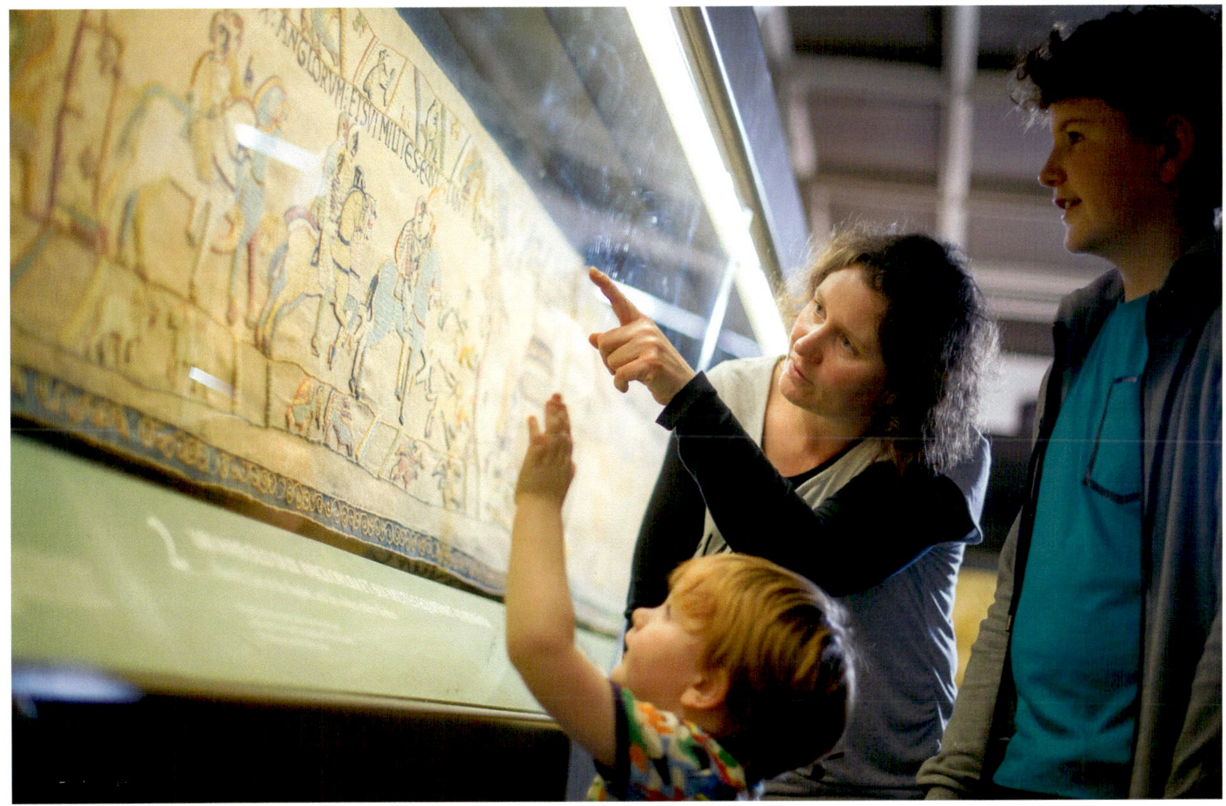

The tapestry, now on permanent display in its purpose-built gallery.

battlefield itself. Occasionally it was placed on temporary exhibition in Reading, though neither here nor at most of its loan exhibition venues was there a gallery large enough to display it adequately.

With the wide programme of restoration and expansion of the museum at Reading in 1993, there was at last the opportunity to display the replica permanently in an appropriate setting. After checking the colour-fastness of the dyes, it was very carefully washed in a solution, then stitched to a support fabric of washed linen, and finally given a lining of linen. It was remounted and set up as a continuous strip in a specially designed and illuminated case. The 25 separate sections have not been physically re-joined for the tapestry's new display.

The story of the tapestry

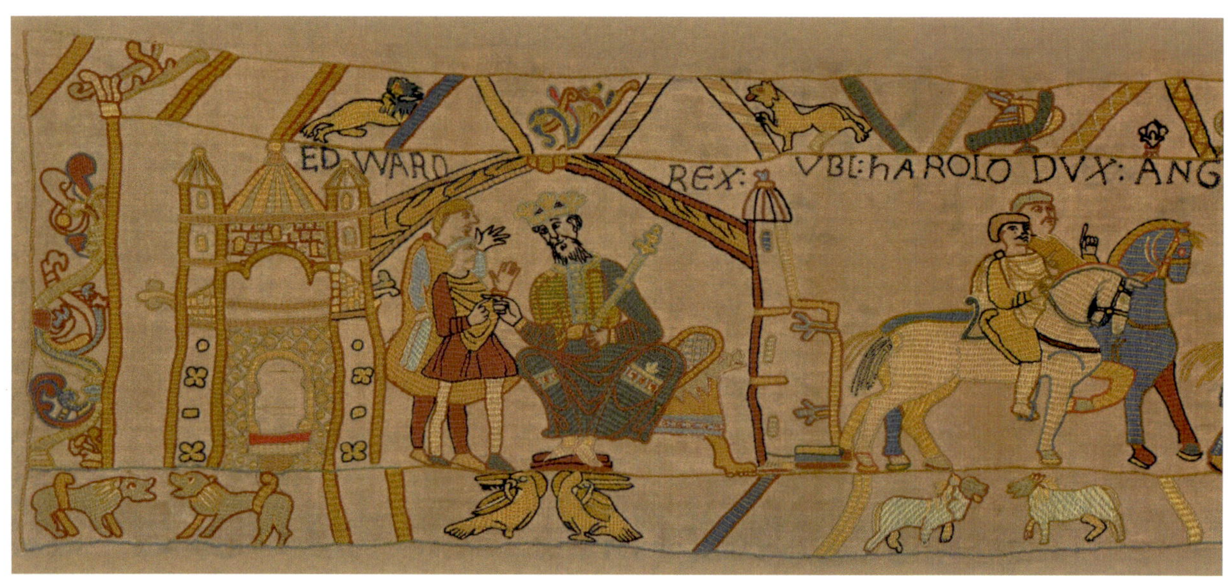

It is 1064. In the Royal Palace of Westminster, Edward the Confessor, king of England since 1042, is instructing his brother-in-law Harold, Earl of Wessex, to inform William, Duke of Normandy, that he is the King's chosen successor to the English throne. (Or perhaps he is advising him not to go to Normandy, see p. 2)

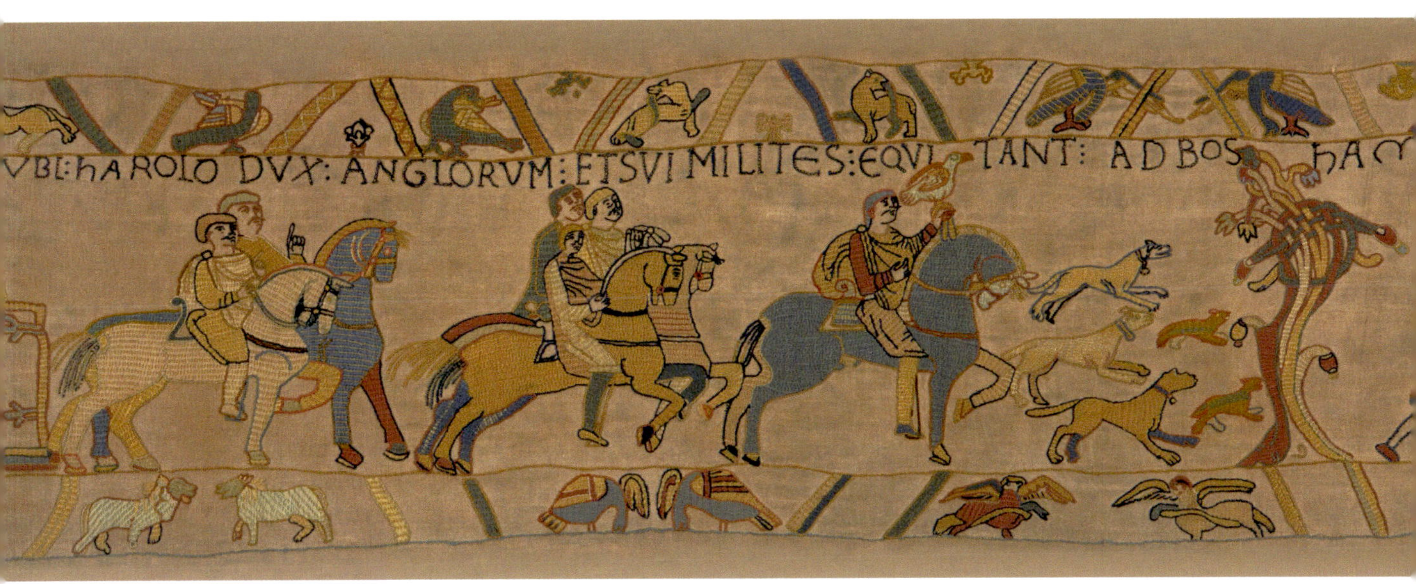

After this, Harold, holding a hawk, makes for the south coast with his followers and hunting dogs. They are heading for Bosham in Sussex, Harold's family
estate.

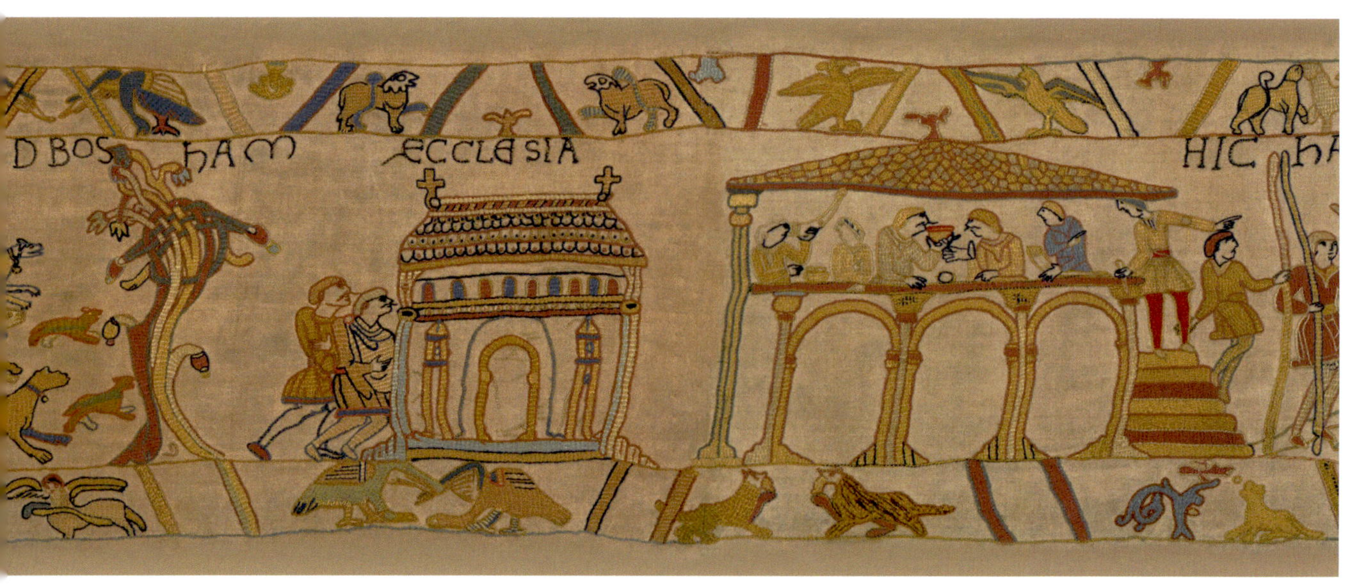

Harold and a companion enter the church at Bosham to pray for a safe voyage. The night before they leave a feast is held in the manor house at Bosham – one of Harold's many houses.

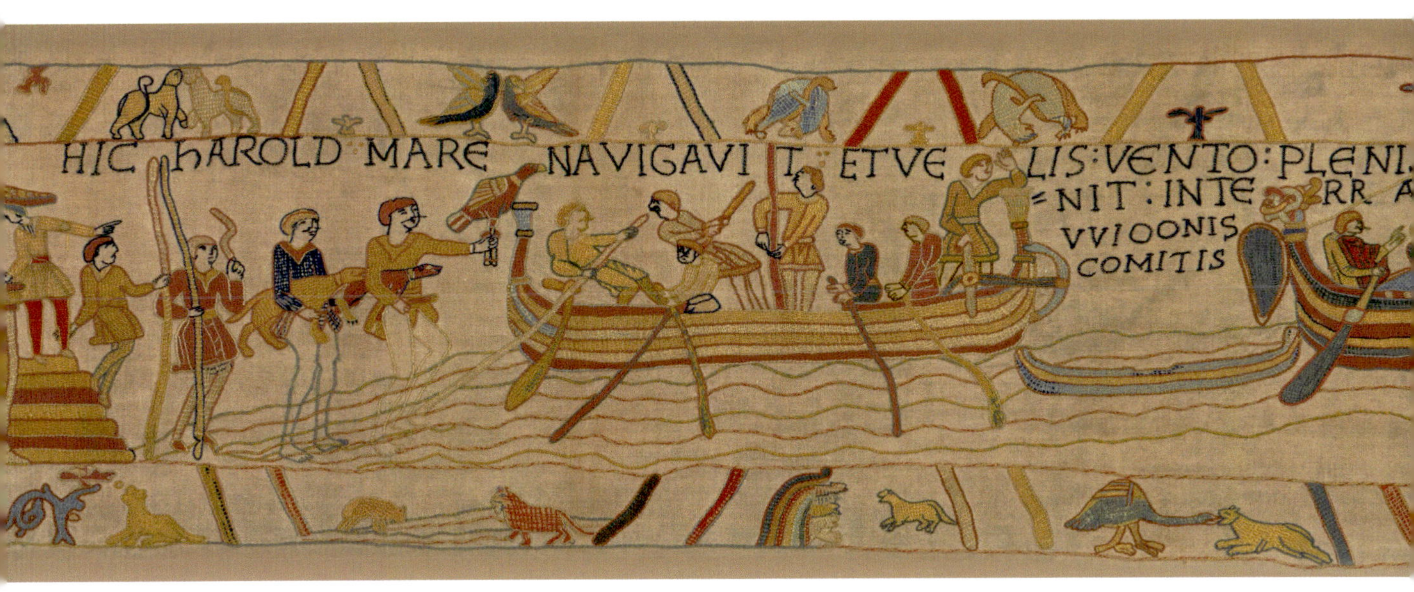

Harold boards his ship and sets sail. He is still carrying his hawk.

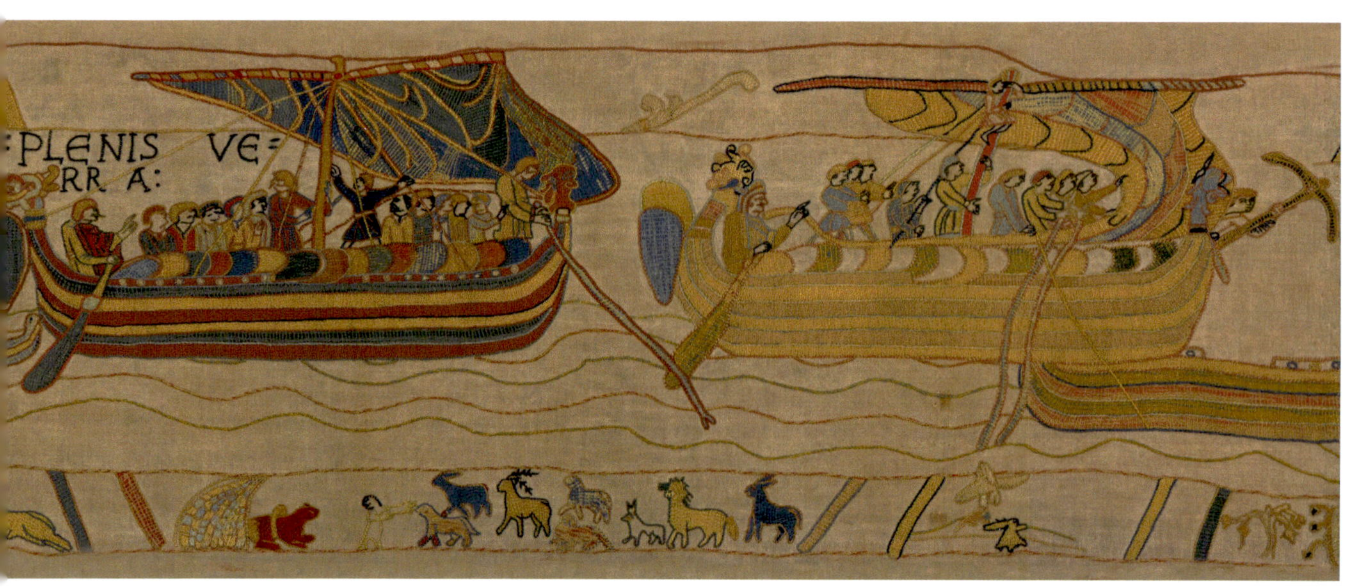

Harold's ship is driven by strong winds across the channel. From the mast a lookout spies land. It is Ponthieu, north of Normandy, the territory of the fierce Count Guy, and the wind, unfortunately, forces his ship aground here.

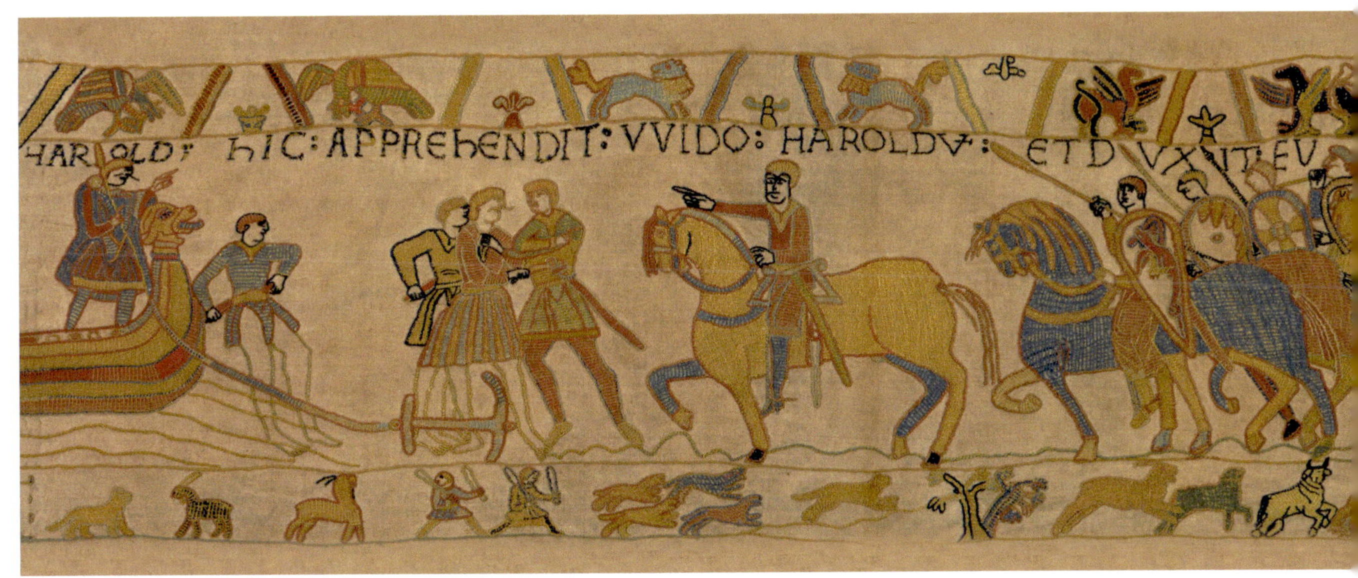

Harold is shown standing on the ship, ready to land. Then, as soon as he climbs down, he is seized by the soldiers of Count Guy, who directs operations from horseback and orders his men to take Harold prisoner.

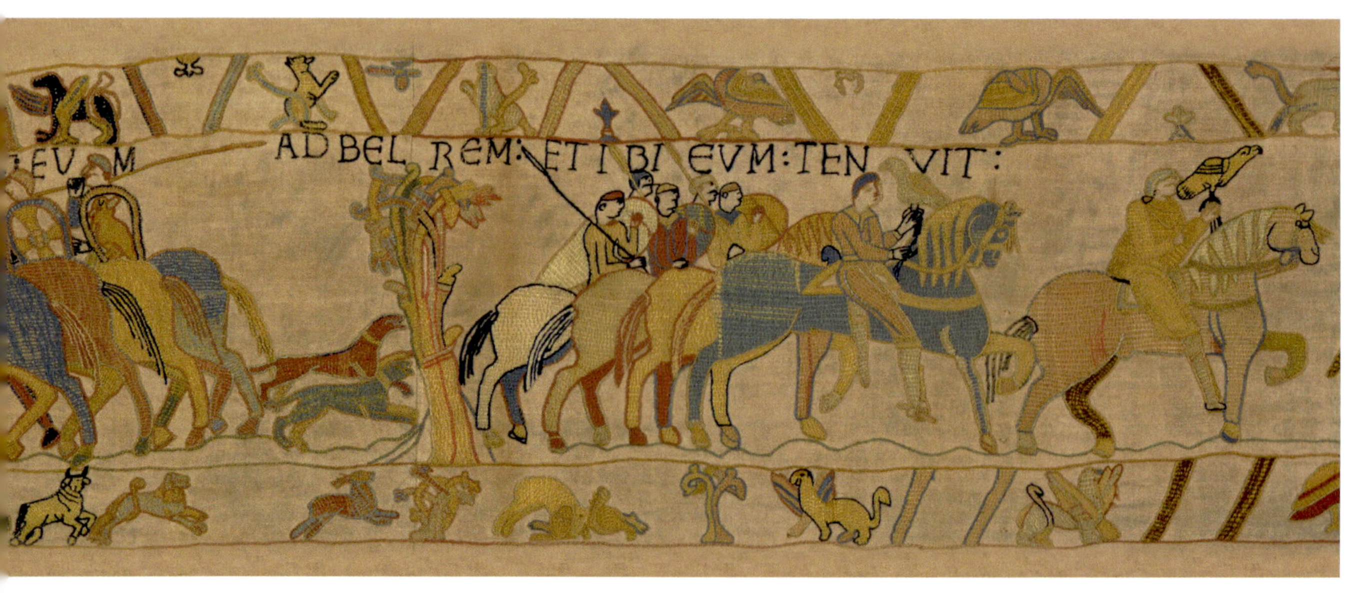

Harold, although a prisoner, is treated with respect; he rides in front of Guy and both are holding hawks as they ride towards Beaurain, Guy's capital town.

Animals in the border

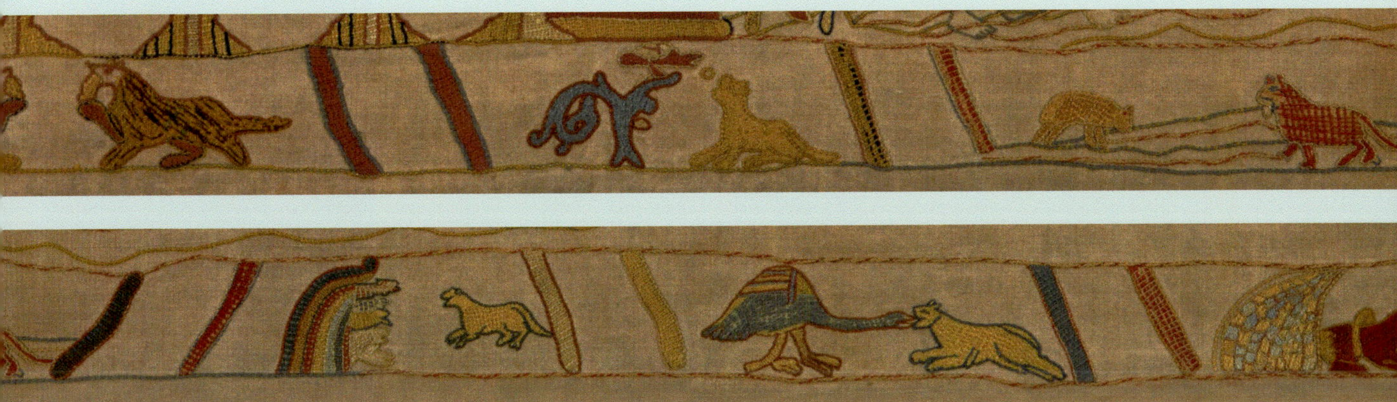

There are 731 animals and birds in the tapestry and the narrow border that runs along the top and bottom is a fascinating accompaniment to the main story. Sometimes the figures and animals seem to bear no relation to the narrative, although there is the possibility that the original embroiderers were adding coded messages to the account. Among the fantastic beasts and birds in this section are a few familiar scenes such as the Fox and the Crow from Aesop's Fables. This story warns against flattery. The crow has found a tasty piece of cheese and retired to his branch to feast on it. The fox, below, wants the cheese for himself and, not being able to climb, resorts to cunning in order to get it. He flatters the crow. He tells the bird how beautiful he is and asks whether his voice is as sweet. Of course, the crow opens his mouth to demonstrate, the cheese falls and the fox gobbles it up.

The very next picture (separated by two slanting lines) depicts Aesop's story of the Wolf and the Lamb, in which the wolf tries to justify its murderous intent by accusing the lamb of all sorts of crimes, all of which the lamb proves it didn't do. In the end the wolf eats the lamb anyway. The moral of the story is that wicked people will not listen to the reasoning of the innocent. Why did the embroiderers include these two stories here and what messages did they intend to convey?

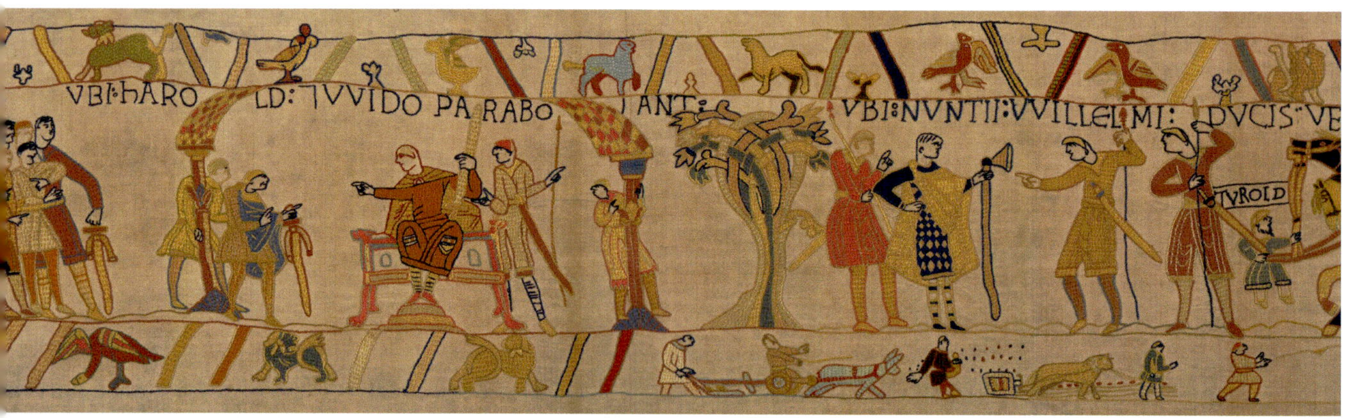

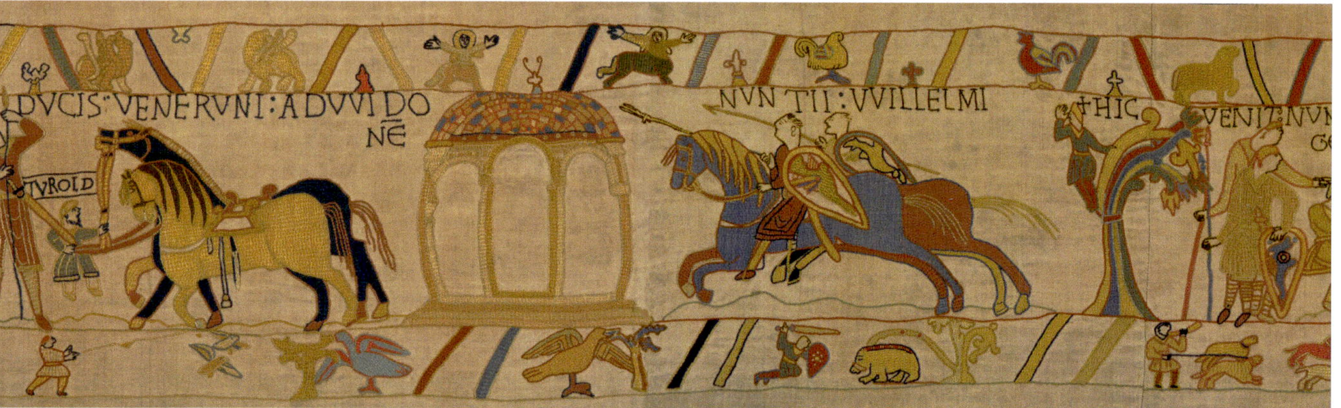

Guy sits on his throne and discusses a ransom with Harold. The next three segments continue the story in reverse order. On the right-hand side of the top section, two messengers arrive from Duke William of Normandy to demand Harold's release. 'Turold' may be the very short figure, or one of the two messengers.

In the second segment the armoured messengers are starting out, riding furiously with their hair flying in the wind to take a message from William to Guy.

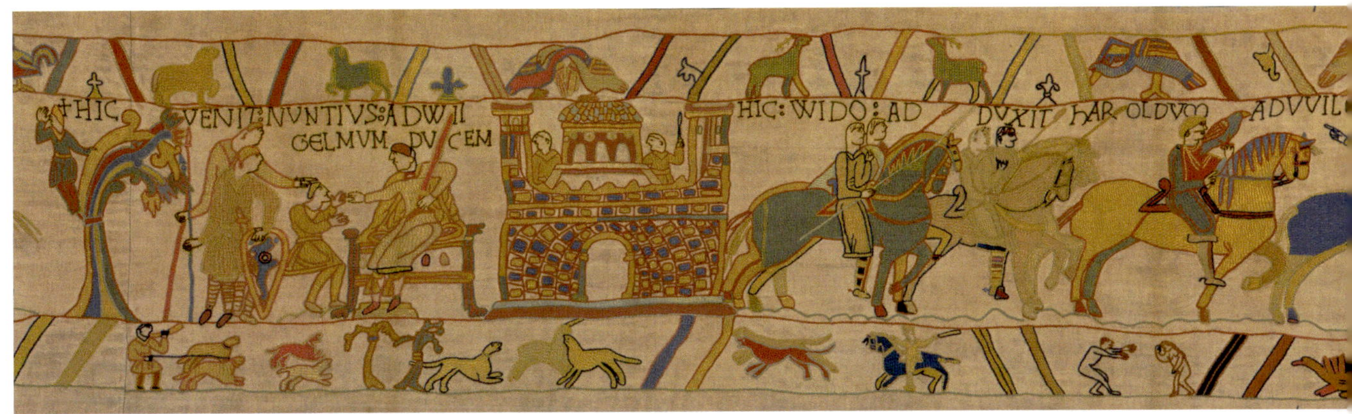

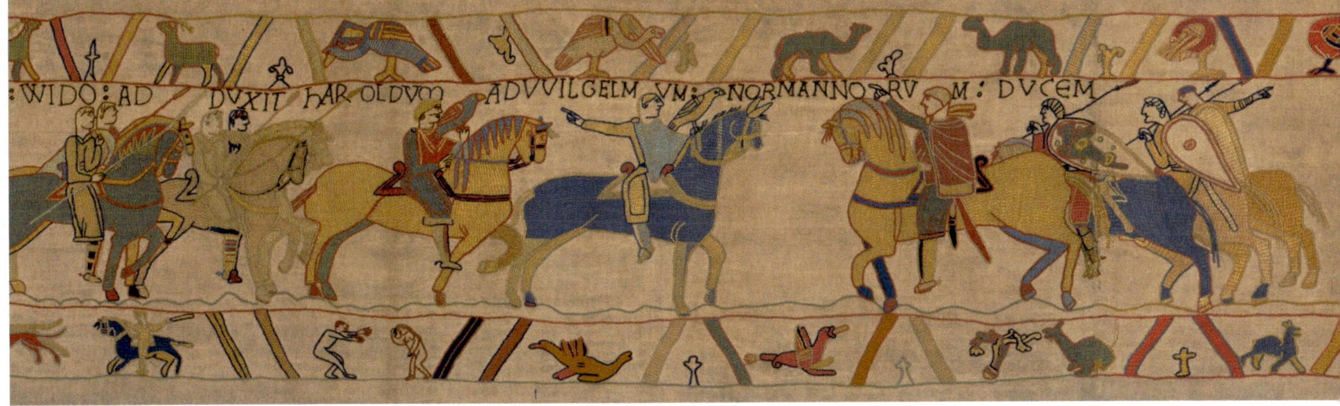

This is really the first of the three segments in terms of order of events. At the top left, news is brought to William that Guy has seized Harold.

Now, having received the message depicted in segment one, Guy obeys William's order and takes Harold to meet him. Guy and William both point to Harold; both Harold and Guy carry their hawks.

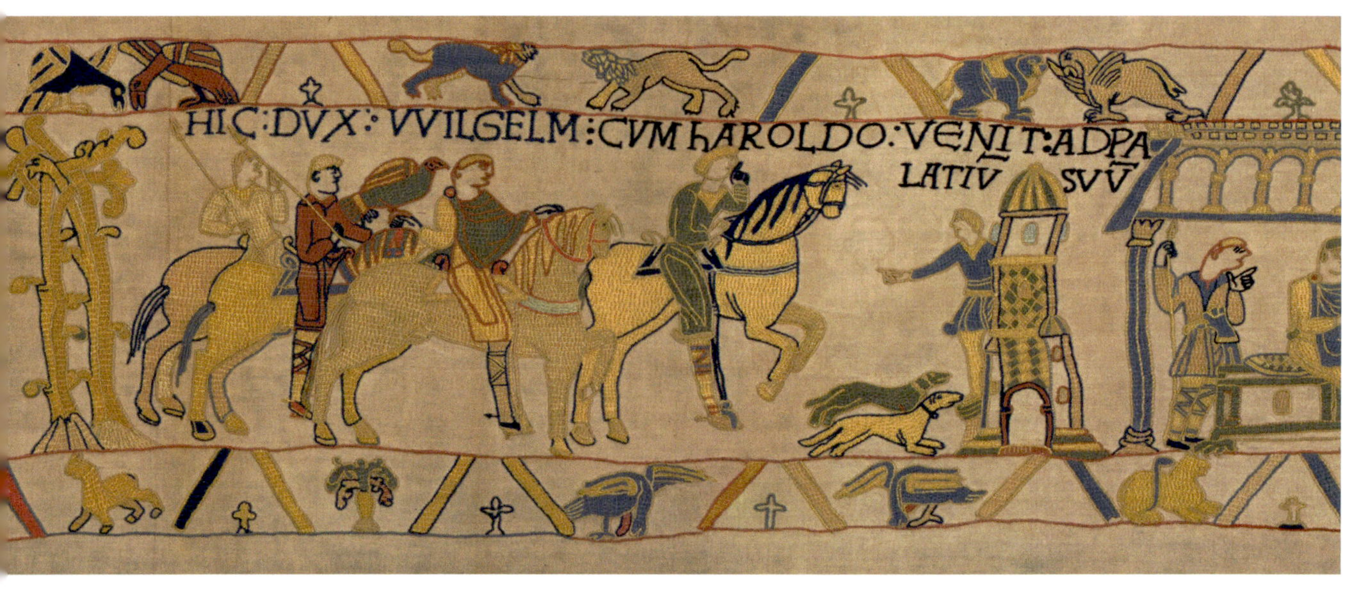

William and Harold ride with soldiers to William's palace at Rouen, arriving at the gate (now William has the hawk!).

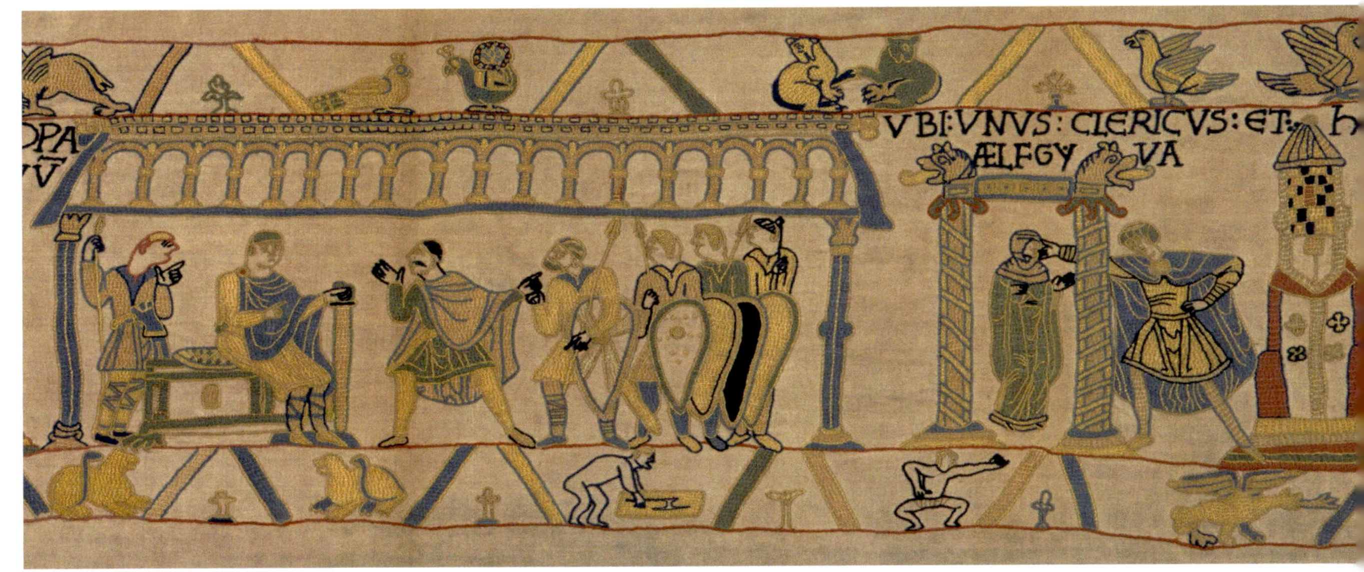

William sits while Harold talks to him.

The mysterious incident on the far right may have nothing to do with the main story, but was probably well known in the 11th century. It might refer to a sexual scandal – the man in the lower border is naked in the original tapestry, but he has been provided with pants in this copy. Alternatively, the woman, named Aelfgyva (one of only three women depicted in the tapestry), may be the subject of William and Harold's discussions. She might have been one of William's daughters or Harold's sister, and it is speculated that the men are discussing her marriage.

Character identification

Eight different colours can be distinguished in the both the original and the replica tapestries: three shades of blue (one is almost black), two greens (one light, one dark), red, a mustard yellow and grey. These colours are used quite arbitrarily, making characters difficult to identify from scene to scene. Some of the horses have different-coloured legs and hooves and some men have blue or green hair. The Latin inscriptions embroidered above and around the pictures help, as do symbols such as God's hand hovering in the sky above Westminster Abbey (below) indicating its holiness, and the man on the left climbing up to set the weathercock in place shows how new it was – it had been consecrated 10 days before Edward's death. The clothing worn by the characters is also indicative of their rank. Men wear tunics and breeches to which a surcoat or mantle is added for those of noble birth. The English are nearly always depicted with moustaches and hair of normal length, while the Normans are clean-shaven and have very short hair with bare necks. Similarly, English horses have their manes 'hogged' (clipped), while Norman horses are generally shown with long manes. The English are never shown fighting on horseback, although Harold rides about on one before the battle. There had been an attempt to introduce cavalry to England ten years earlier, but the army had rejected it as 'un-English'!

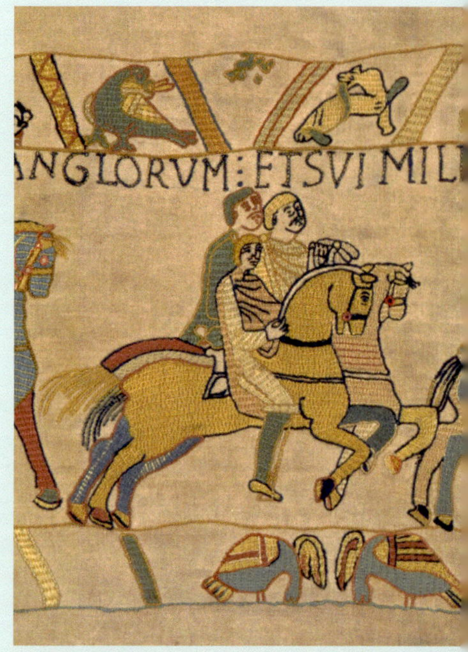

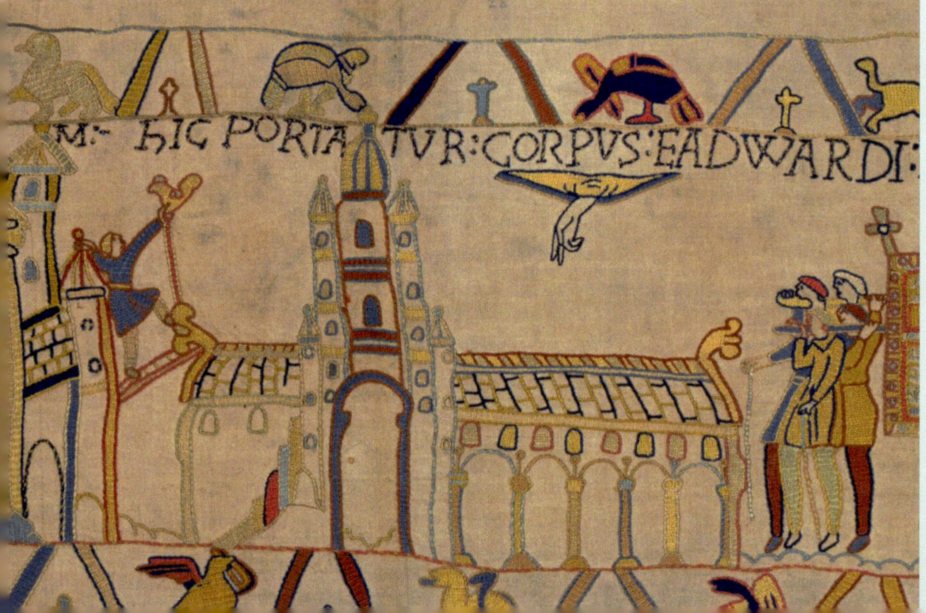

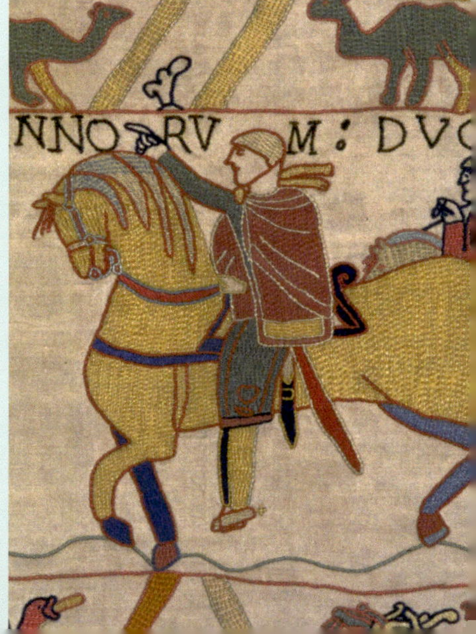

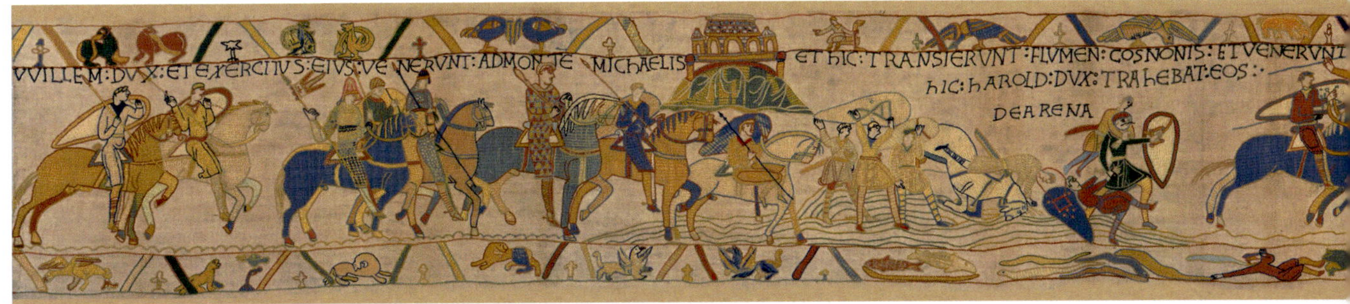

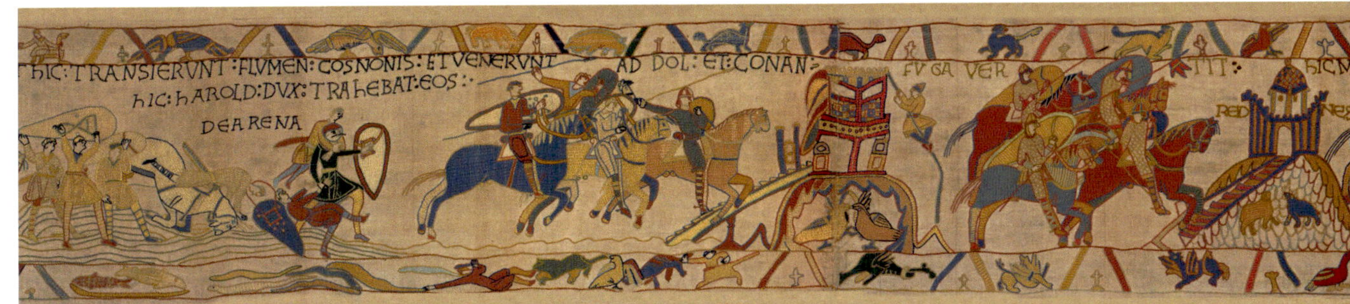

Harold accompanies William and the Norman soldiers as they set off to fight Duke Conan of Brittany, who has declared war on William. They pass Mont Saint Michel, which is on the border between Normandy and Brittany. To get into Brittany they have to cross the Couesnon river. They hold their shields above their heads to keep them out of the water. Some soldiers and horses sink into quicksand and Harold rescues them – two at a time!

The Norman soldiers march into Dol and Duke Conan escapes down a rope from the castle. Chasing Conan, the Normans pass Rennes, the capital of Brittany. Take a look at the images in the lower border here, where a man-beast appears to be holding the tail of a mythical animal, who is in turn biting the wing of a large bird who pecks at the tail of a lion who bites the foot of a man who is attempting to hold onto a slippery eel. What message were the embroiderers conveying here?

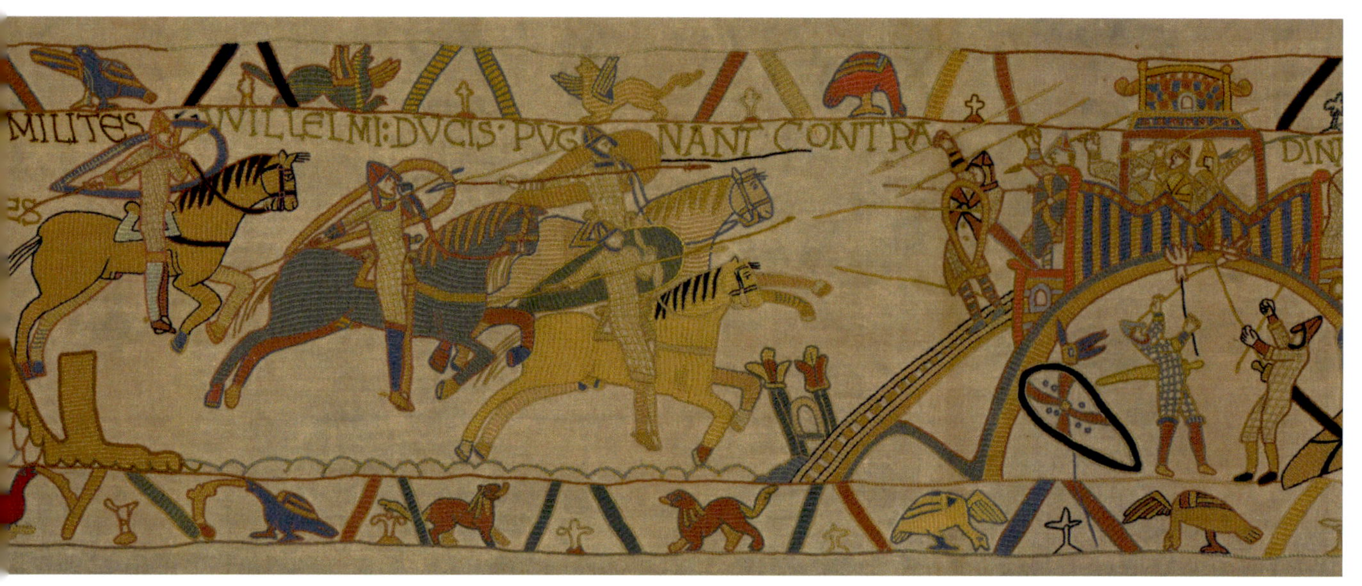

The Normans catch up with Conan at Dinan. During the battle, soldiers on horseback throw lances and others try to set fire to the defences.

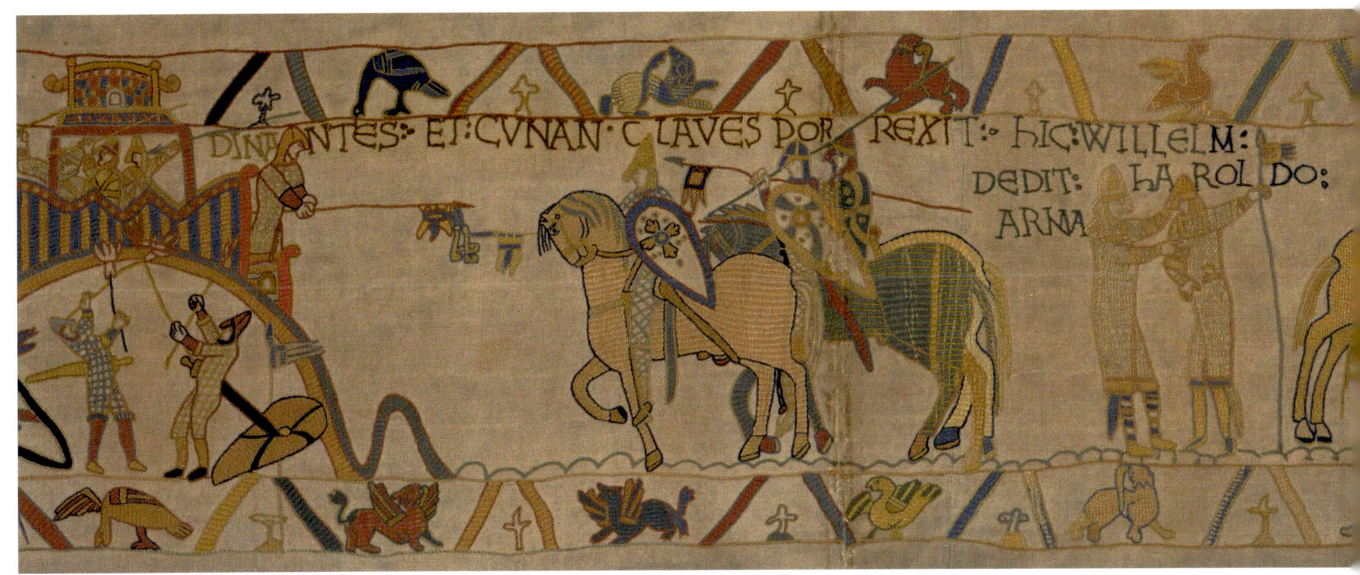

Conan surrenders. He passes the keys of Dinan to William on the point of a lance. As a reward for his services, William honours Harold with the gift of arms. This ceremony would have been seen as making William Harold's overlord – an important event from the Norman point of view.

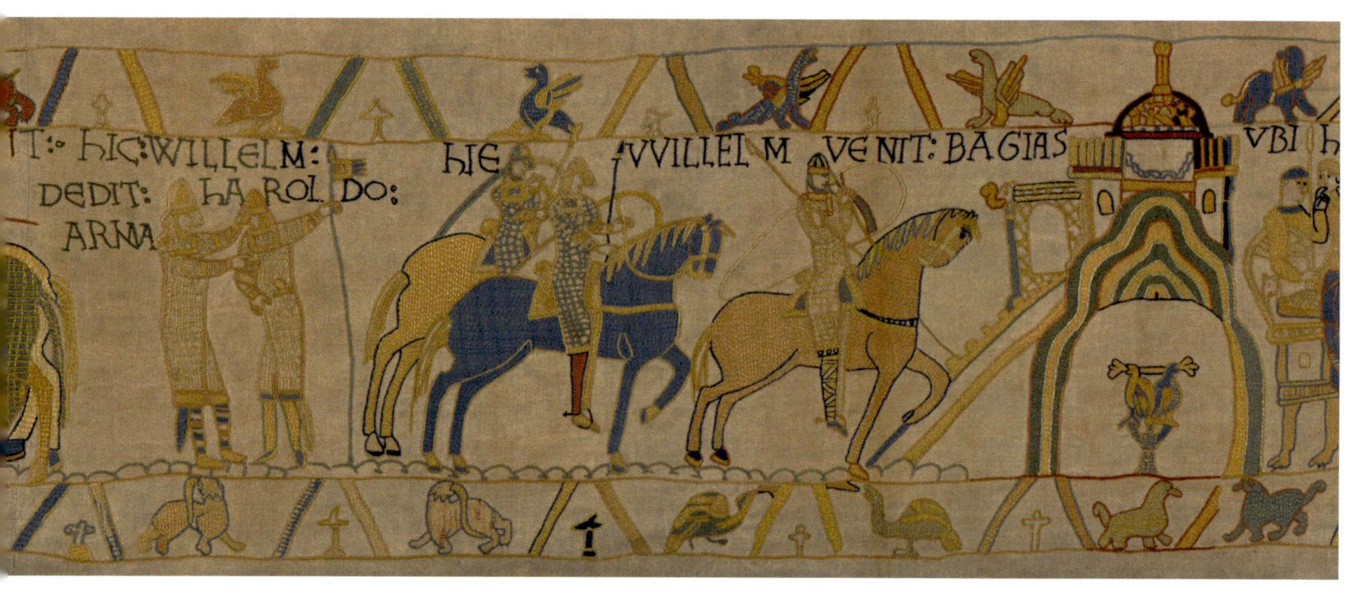

William and Harold return to Normandy and reach the town of Bayeux.

28

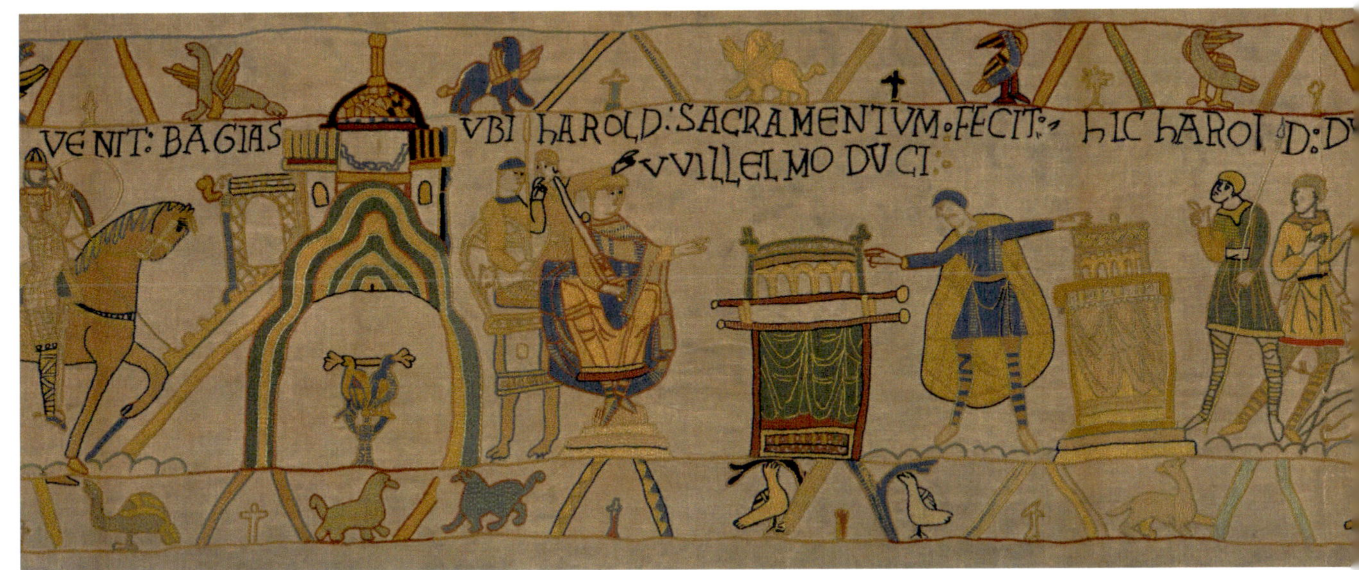

In the climax of the story so far, Harold swears a solemn oath, touching two reliquaries. Was Harold promising to support William?

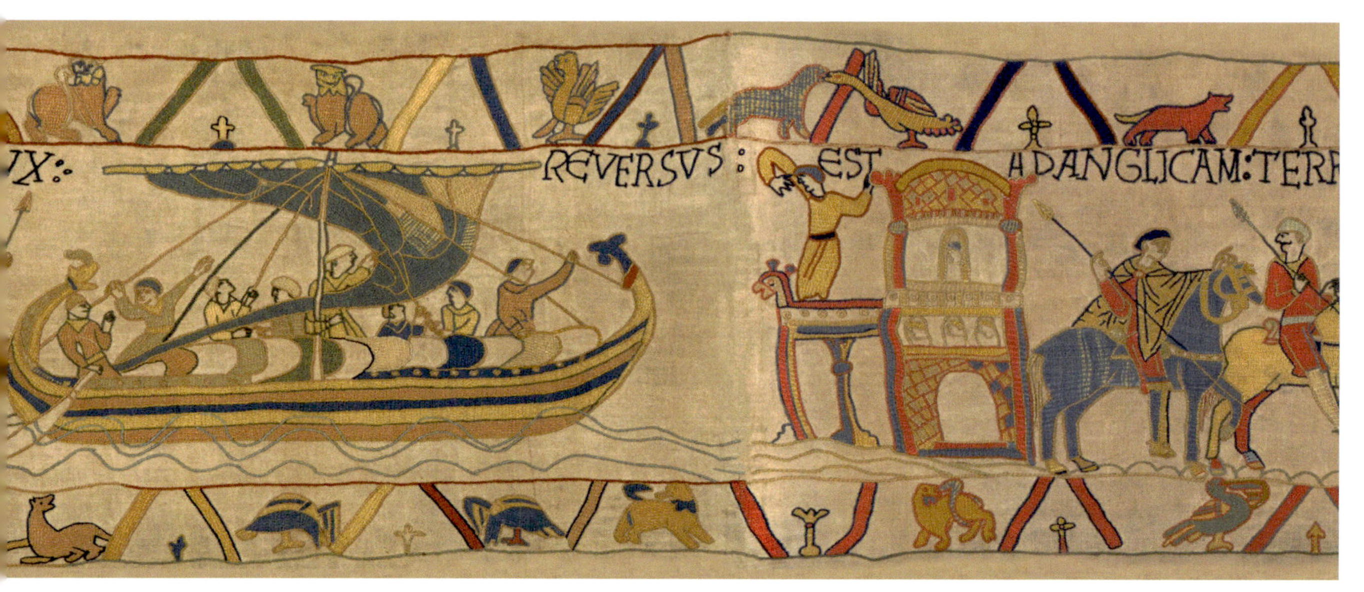

Harold is at last set free and sails back to England.

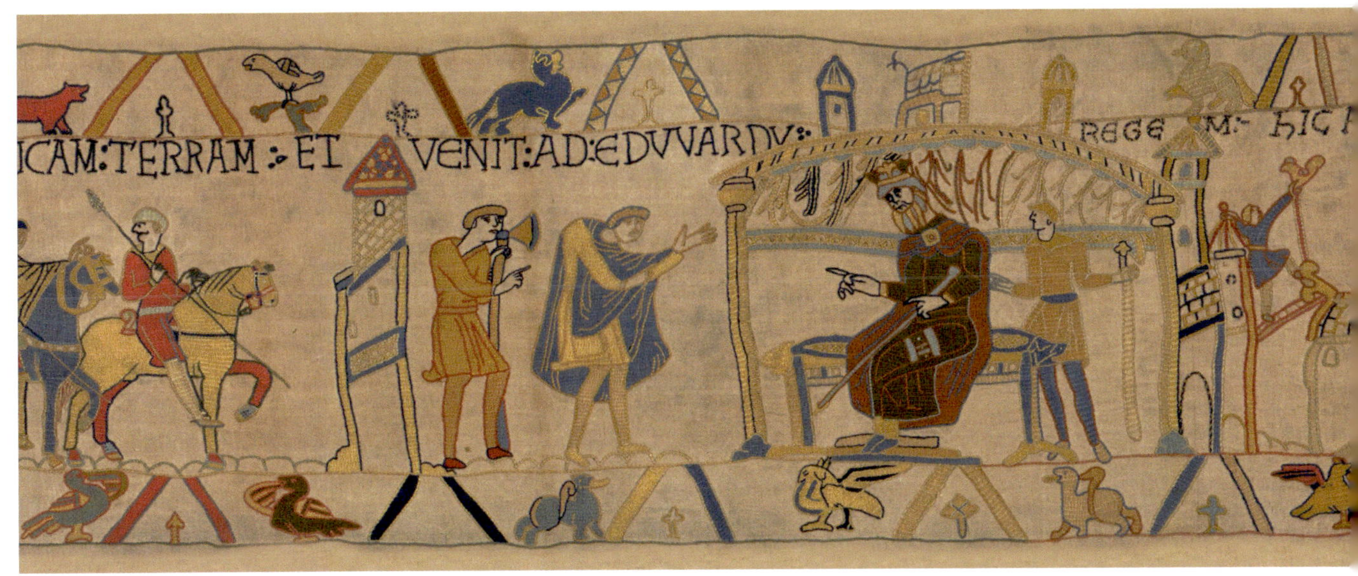

Harold reports to King Edward on his mission to Normandy. The King is shown as frail and ill, although he was in fact perfectly healthy at this time.

The three kings in the tapestry

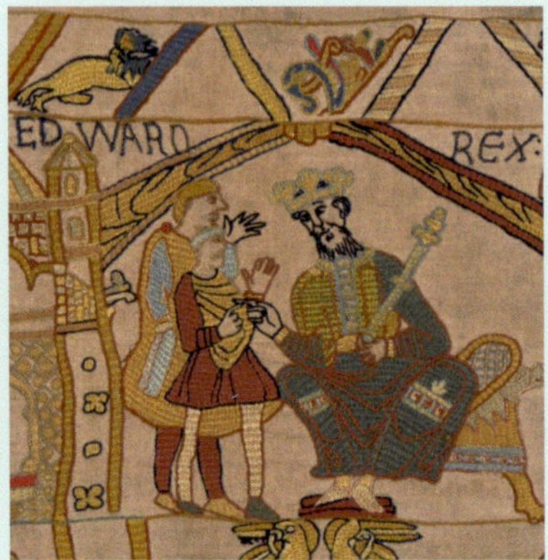

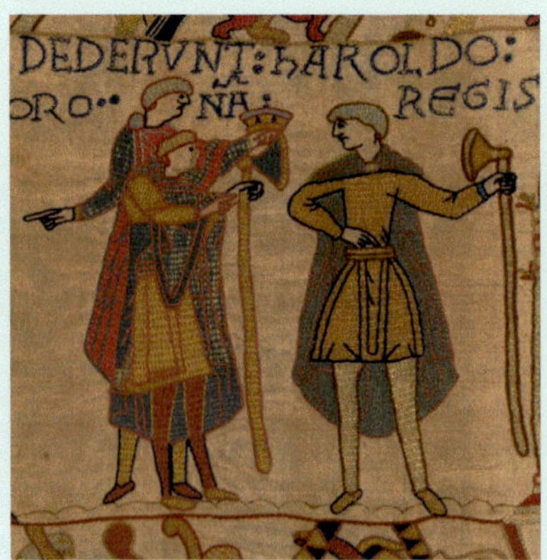

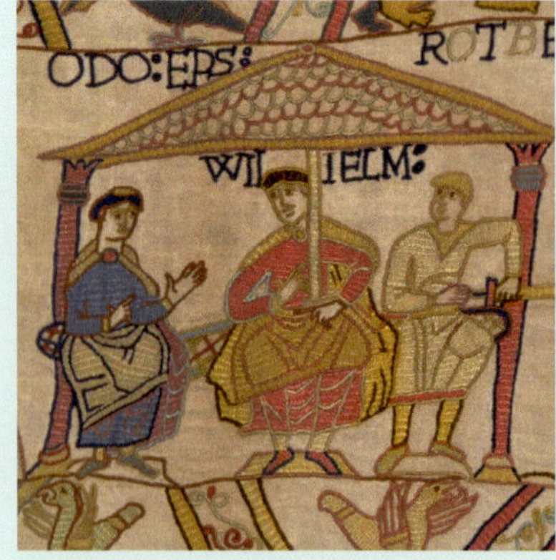

Edward the Confessor, king of England 1042–1066. Edward died without children, leaving several candidates with claims to the throne. His reputation as a saintly, pro-Norman ruler seems to have been post-Conquest propaganda.

Harold, king of England 1066. Edward's brother-in-law. Nominated by Edward as his successor, Harold was supported by both lay people and the clergy in England.

William of Normandy, king of England 1066–1087. Edward's cousin's son. William became king after the death of Harold at the battle of Hastings. However, opposition to him, both in England and on the Continent, continued sporadically throughout his reign.

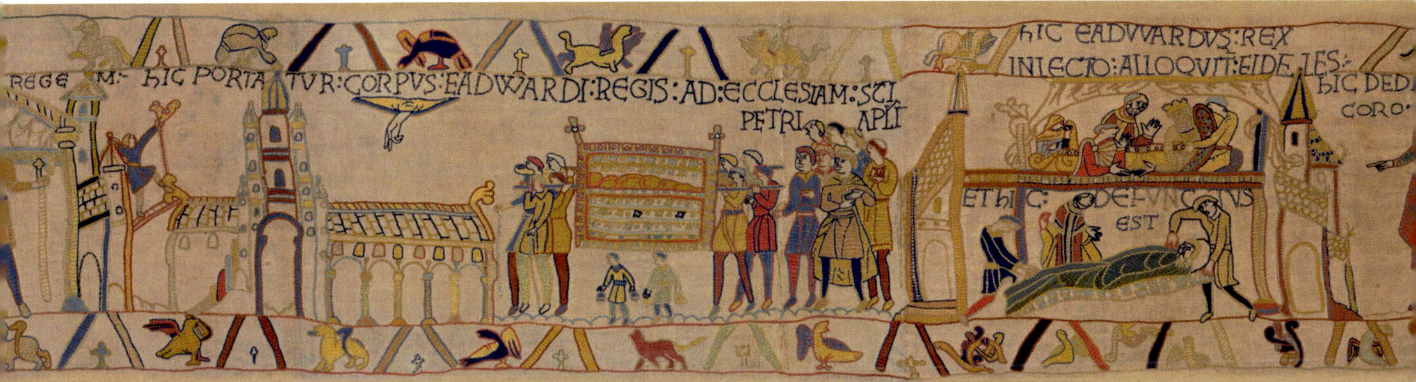

Edward died on 5 January 1066. The tapestry reverses the scenes of his death and his burial. On the right, in the upper chamber, King Edward is in his bed talking to his faithful followers, including Harold and Queen Edith – below he is shown dead with a priest in attendance.

In the middle we see his funeral procession to Westminster Abbey, which he had just had built in Norman style (replacing an old Saxon church on the site) and dedicated to St Peter in order to honour a promise to the Pope. Edward had been too ill to attend its consecration on 28 December 1065. (Henry III demolished Edward's abbey and replaced it with the current gothic abbey in 1245.)

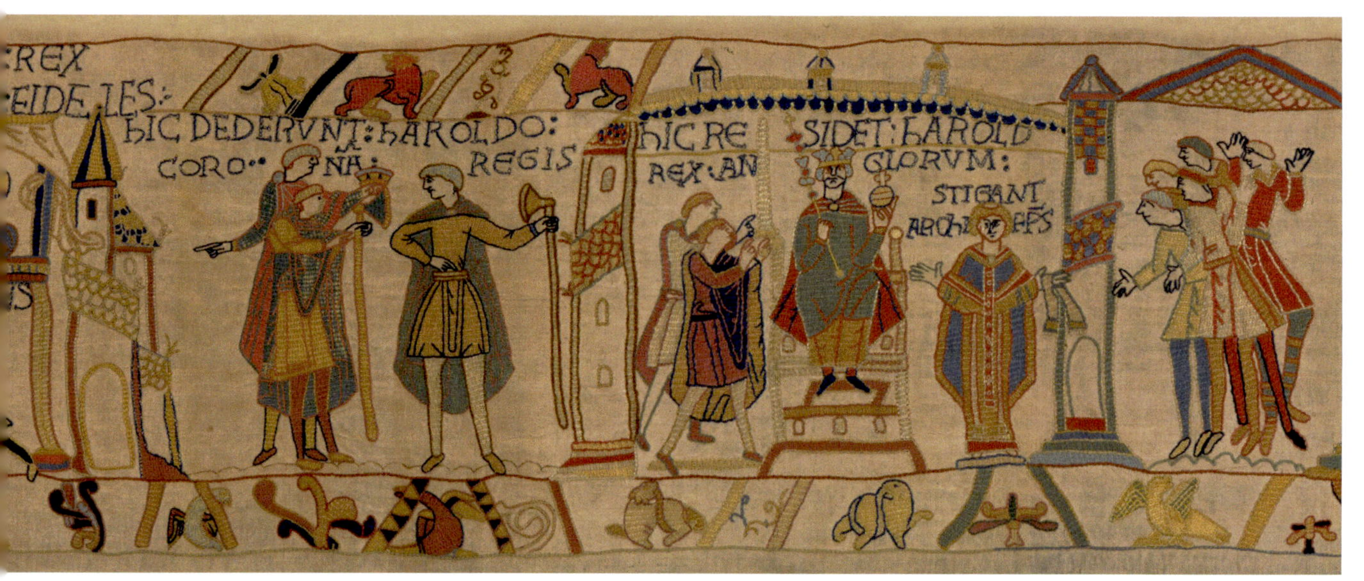

Two noblemen offer Harold the crown and axe, symbols of royal authority, that will make him king. He accepts the offer. Harold is crowned king of England on 6 January 1066, receiving the orb and sceptre. Edward's funeral was that very morning. The new king sits on a throne with nobles to the left and Archbishop Stigand to the right. At the far side, people cheer him.

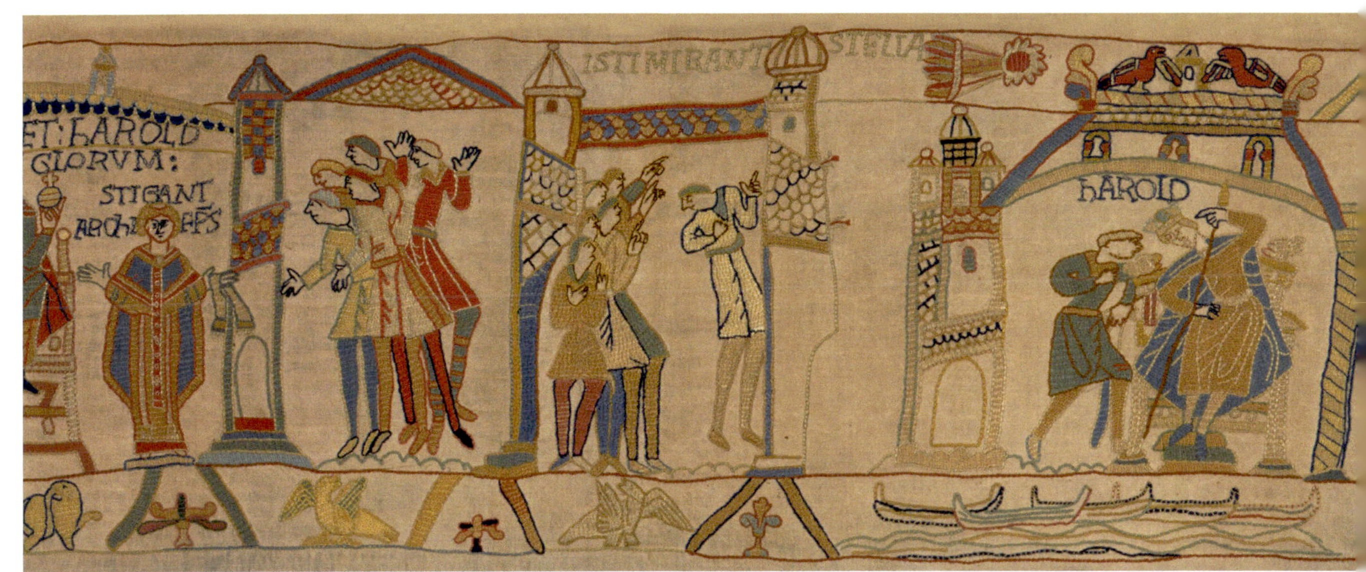

On the far right, Halley's comet appears; people think it is an evil omen and are terrified. News of the comet is brought to Harold; beneath him a ghostly fleet of ships appears in the lower border – a hint of the Norman invasion to come.

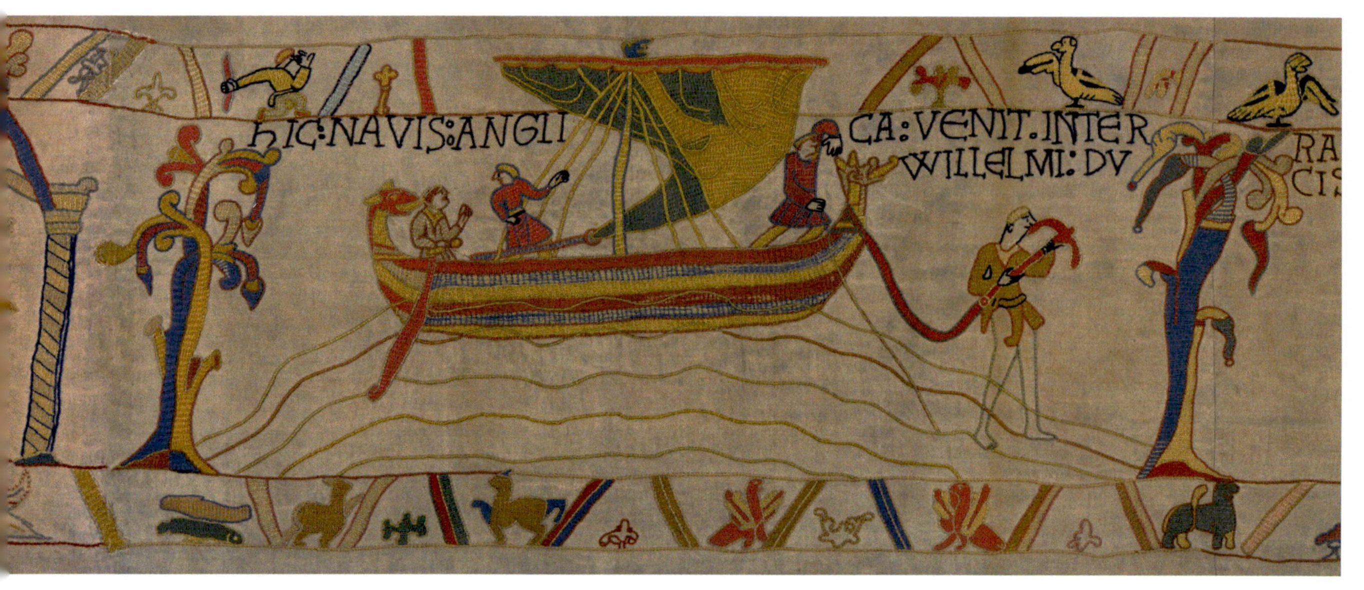

Norman spies carry news of Edward's death and Harold's coronation across the channel to William, Duke of Normandy.

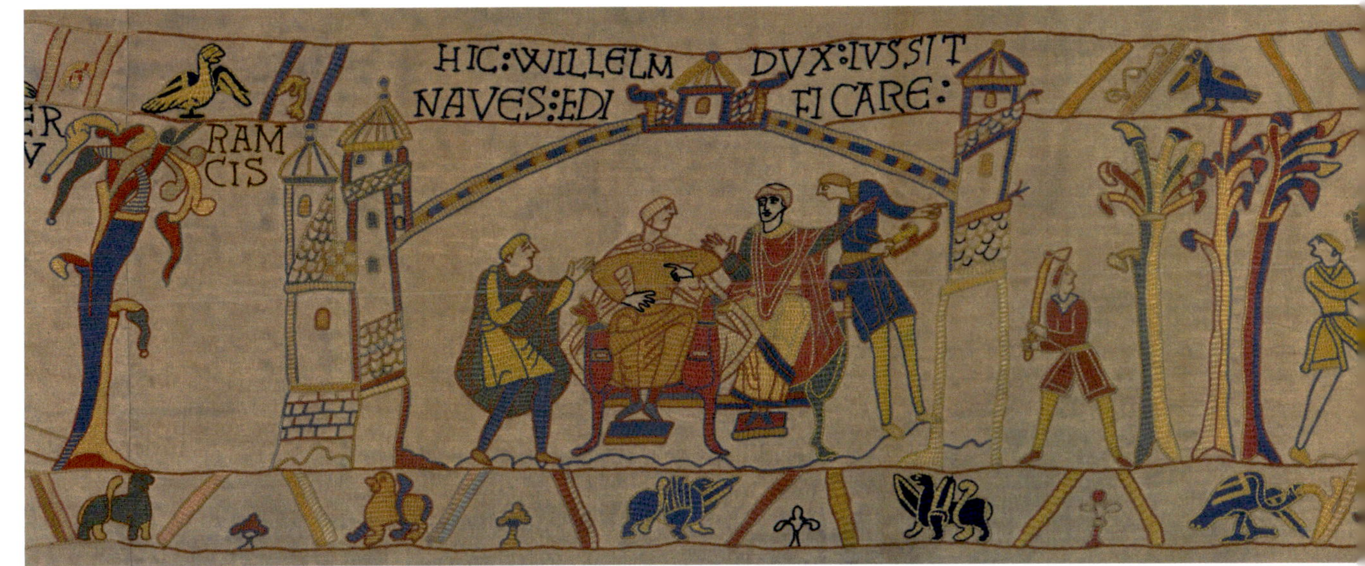

William is furious–he claimed that the throne of England should be his and saw Harold as a usurper. William decides to attack England and orders construction of a fleet of warships. To his left sits Bishop Odo of Bayeux, his half-brother, making his first appearance in the tapestry.

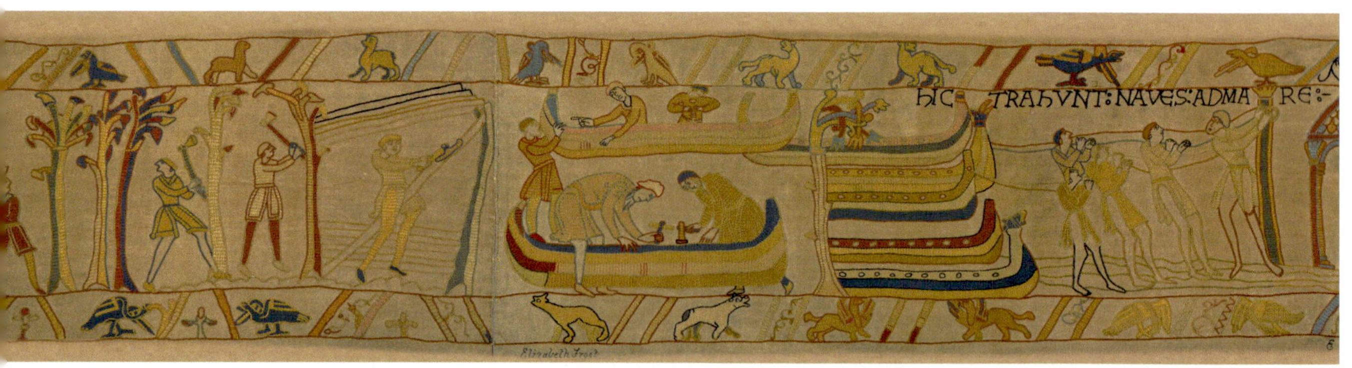

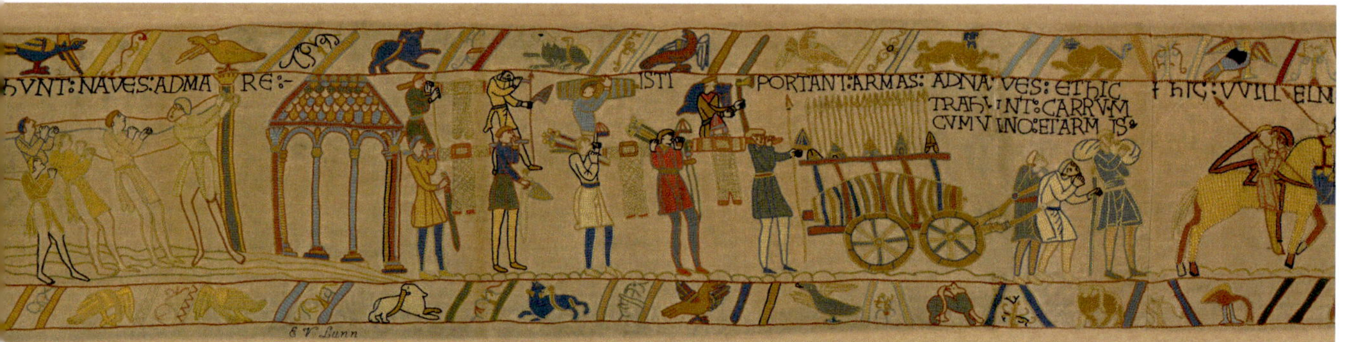

The fleet is built and launched.

Food and drink are taken to the boats, as are weapons: coats of chain mail, helmets, swords and lances.

Unwitting evidence in the Bayeux Tapestry

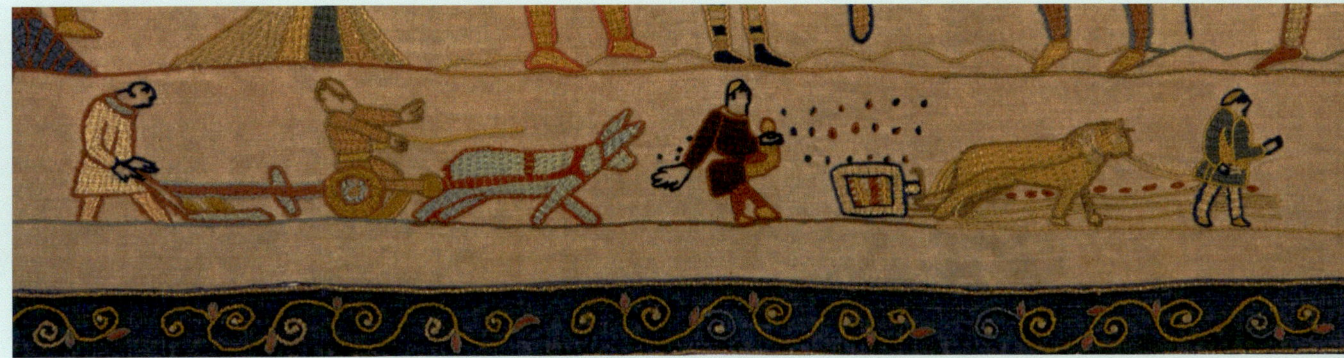

Like any historical artefact or document, both the original Bayeux Tapestry and Reading's replica contain 'unwitting evidence'–clues that tell us about life at the time the story was told. The images in the tapestry are useful to historians as they depict contemporary costume and armour, farming techniques, weapons, boat building, navigation skills, and even the development of castles. The style of the illustration suggests the designer was English as the images are similar to those of contemporaneous Anglo-Saxon manuscripts. The Latin inscriptions look as though they too were commissioned from an English scholar, as proper names are mostly spelt in an English way. The name Gyrth is spelt with a barred D for 'th'–a form of the runic letter *thorn*. There are also quite a few mistakes in the Latin and William's name in its Latin form is spelt in four different ways!

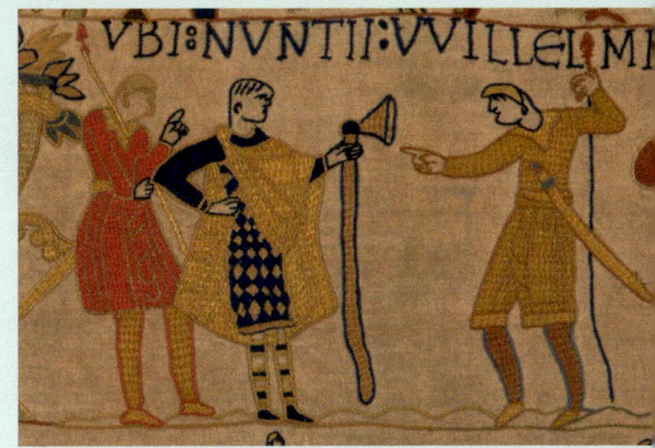

Most of this evidence comes from the Norman original, but the replica also contains clues about its Victorian makers. The Reading copy can be studied to look at the embroidery techniques and the thread dyes used by the Victorians who faithfully copied the original design. However, a nude figure has been given underwear and others have had their genitals removed–changes which were made by the men who hand-coloured the photographs at the South Kensington Museum, not by the embroiderers (see p. 4)–which tells us something about society's values at the time.

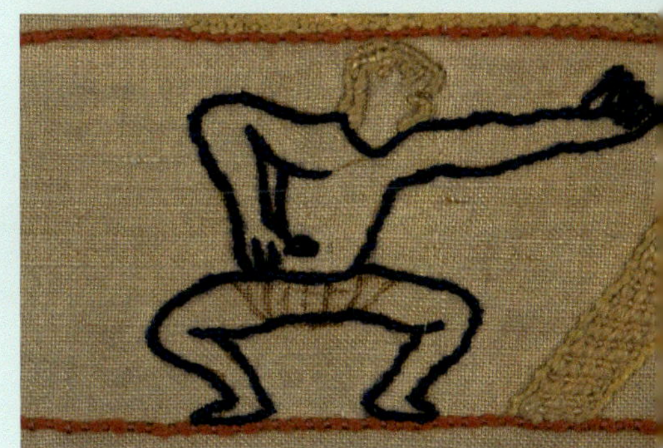

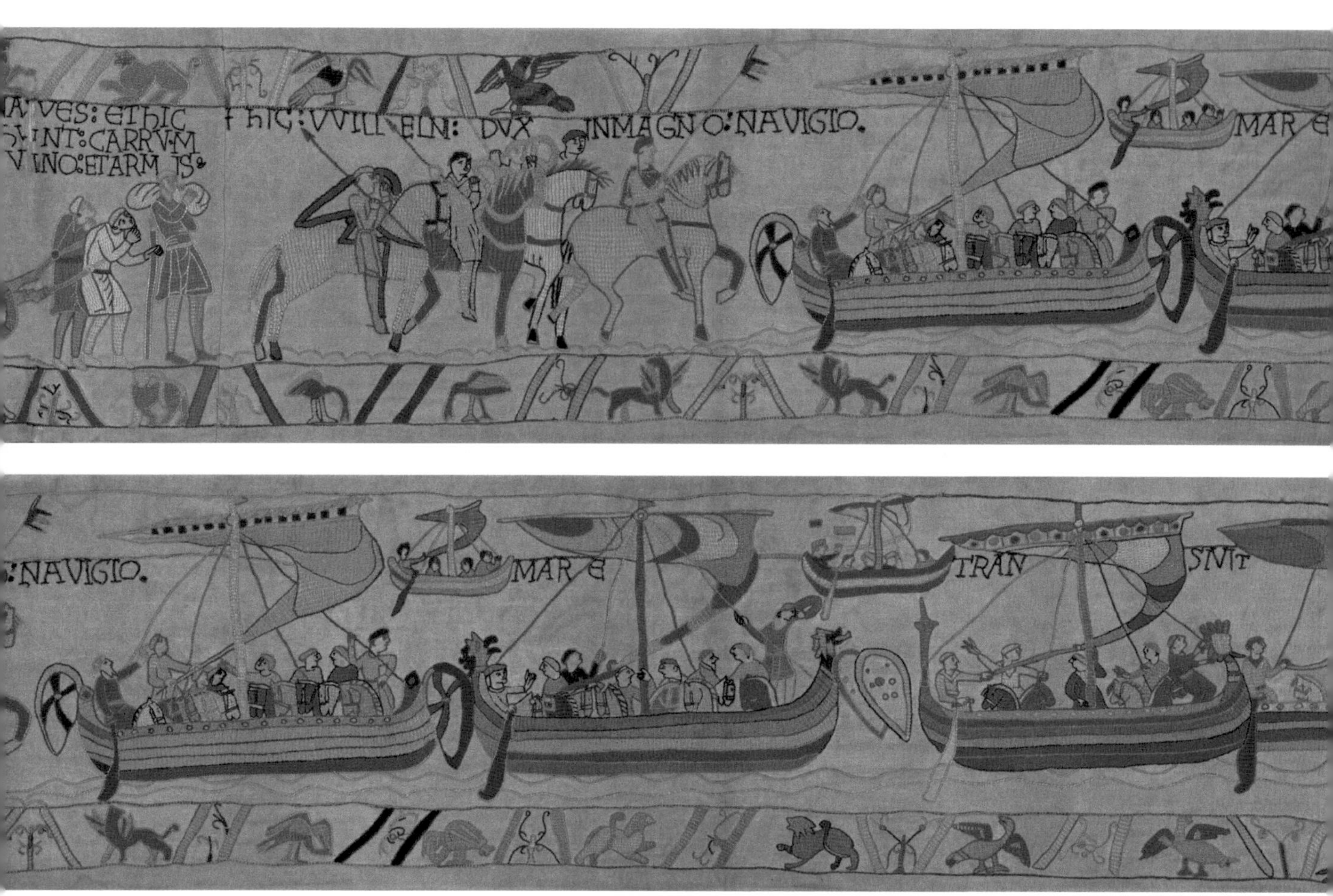

William leads his army to the boats; they embark and set sail.

William sails in the ship Mora, bought for him by his wife Matilda.

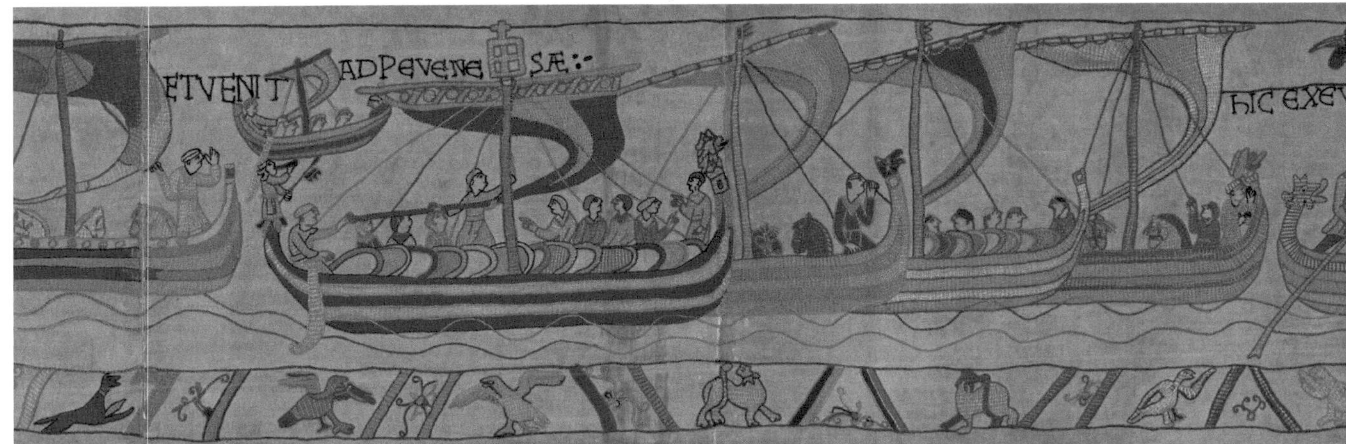

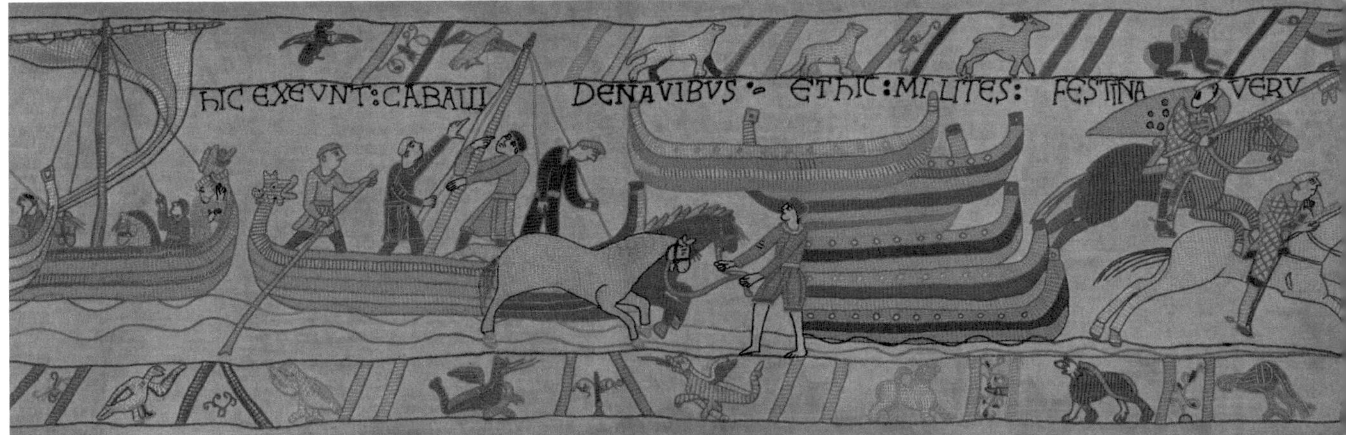

The fleet is a large one.

The duke's ship lands at Pevensey on 28 September and the men disembark the horses.

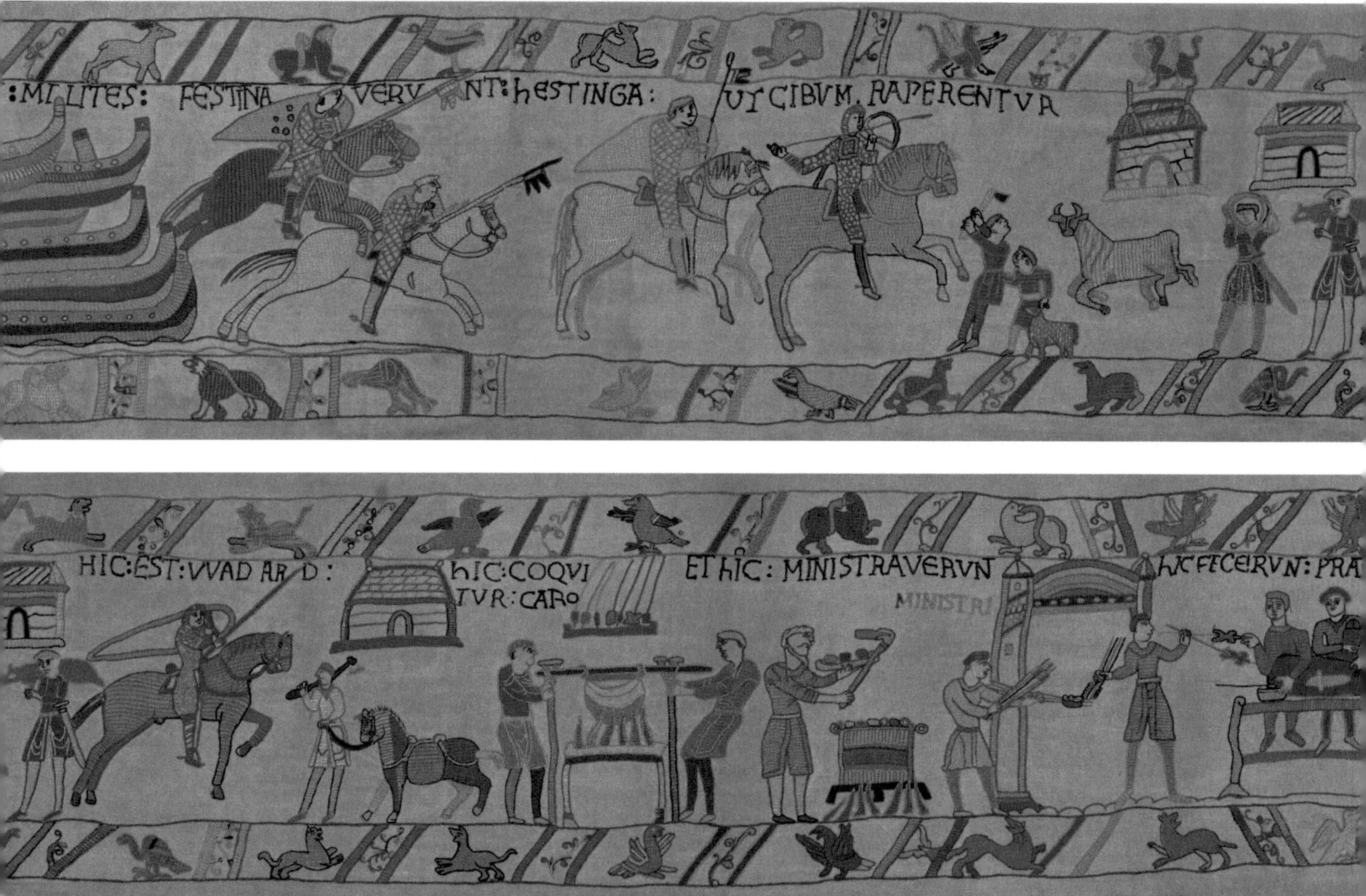

Soldiers ride off towards Hastings and gather food.

Wadar (on the horse, identified by the Latin *HIC:EST:VVAD AR D* above his head), one of William's superintendents and a follower of Bishop Odo, supervises the cooks. The servants bring in roasted meat and fowl. A feast is prepared in the open air – chickens on skewers, a stew cooked over an open fire and food from an outdoor oven.

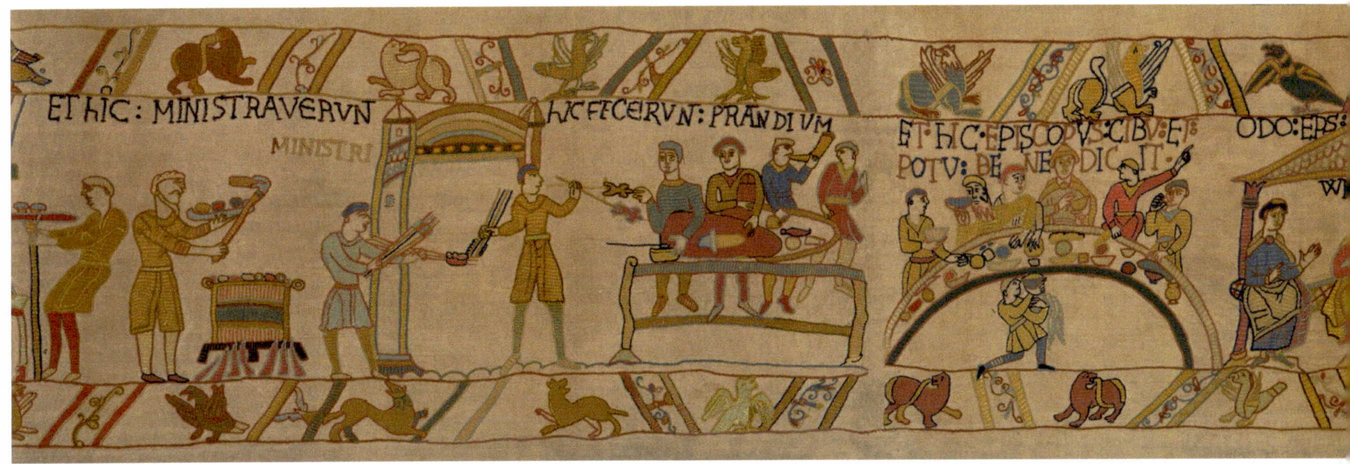

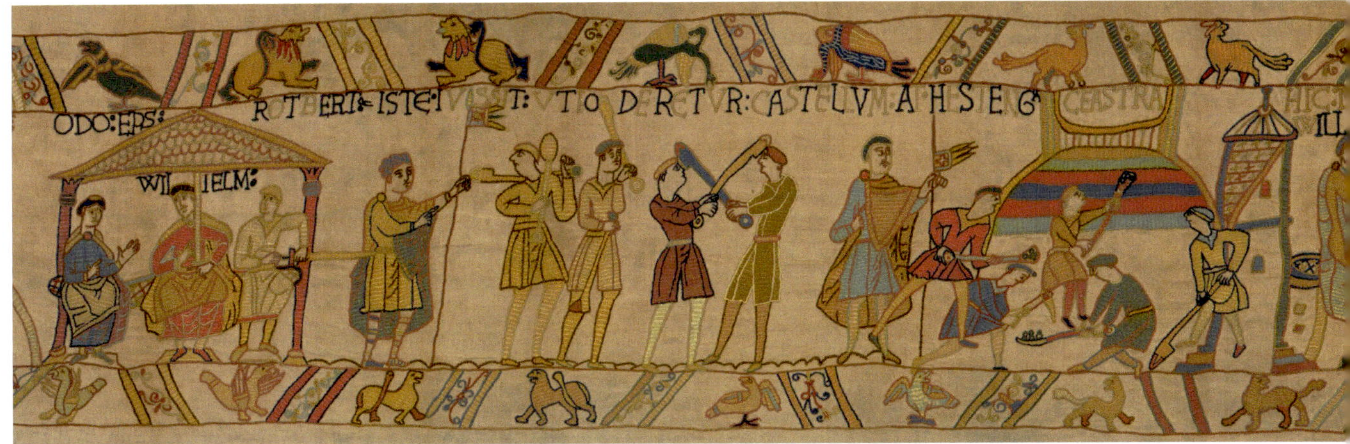

William sits down to a feast with his nobles and Bishop Odo says grace. Servants load food onto shields to carry it to the banquet.

Duke William appears in discussion with his half-brothers Odo and Robert, Count of Mortain. A motte, a defensive mound for a castle, is built to strengthen the Norman invaders' base at Hastings.

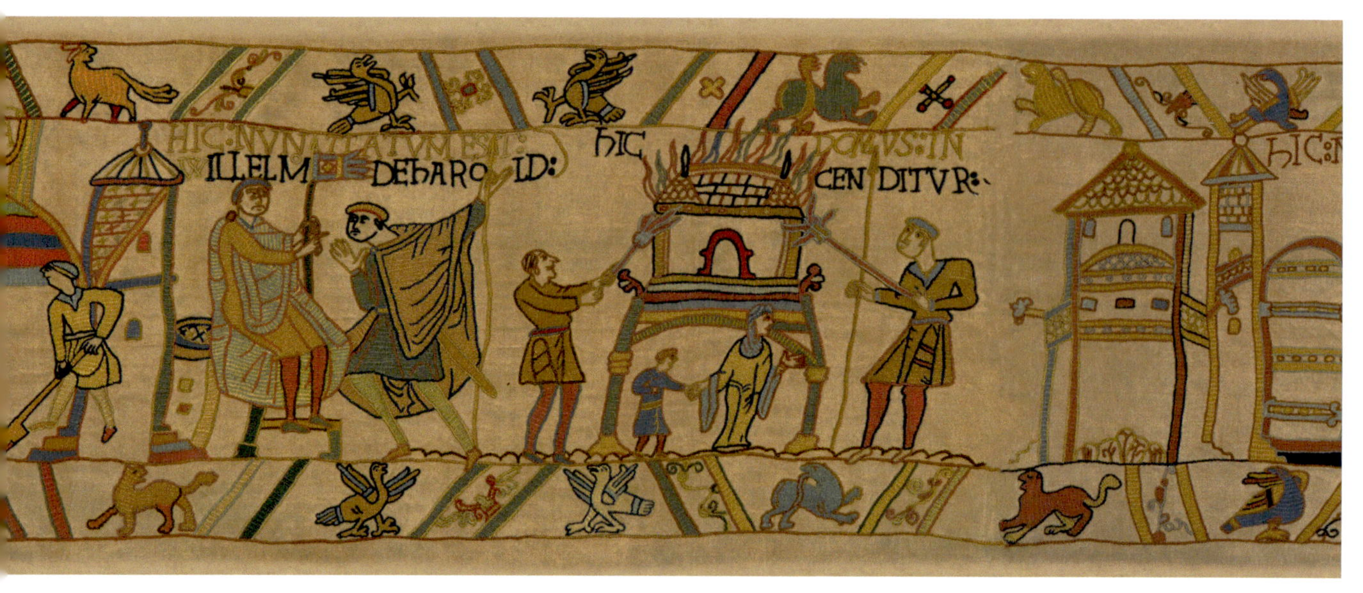

A messenger brings William news of Harold and his army. On the right a woman and her child flee from a burning house.

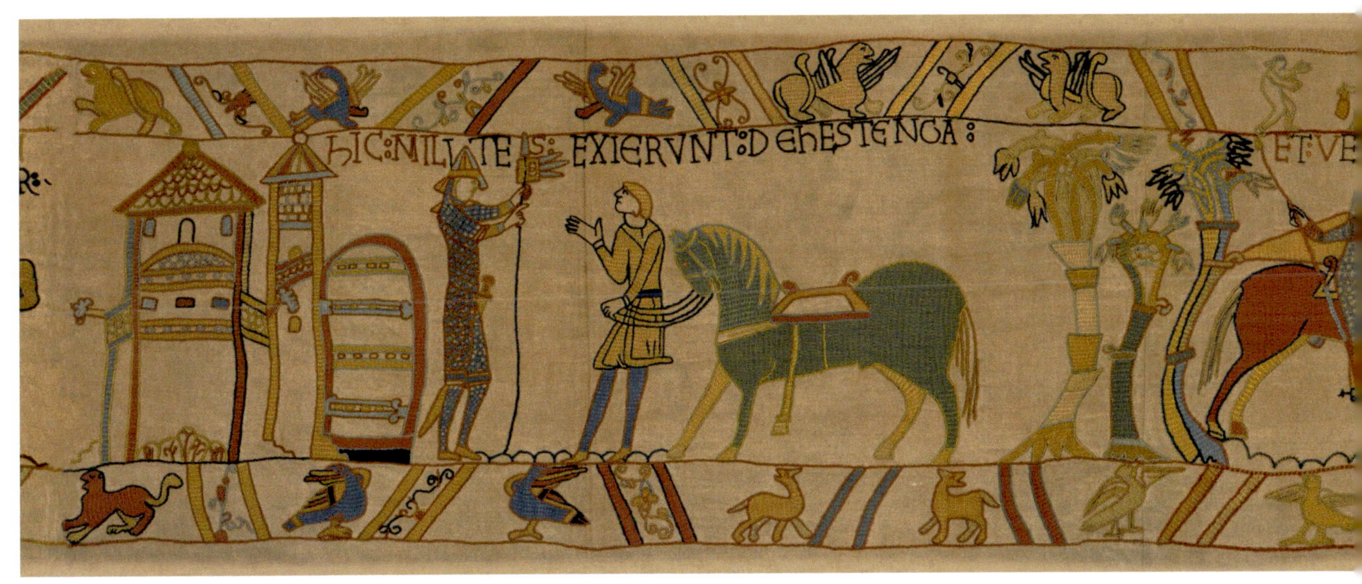

On the morning of the battle, 14 October 1066, William, in full armour, is about to mount his horse.

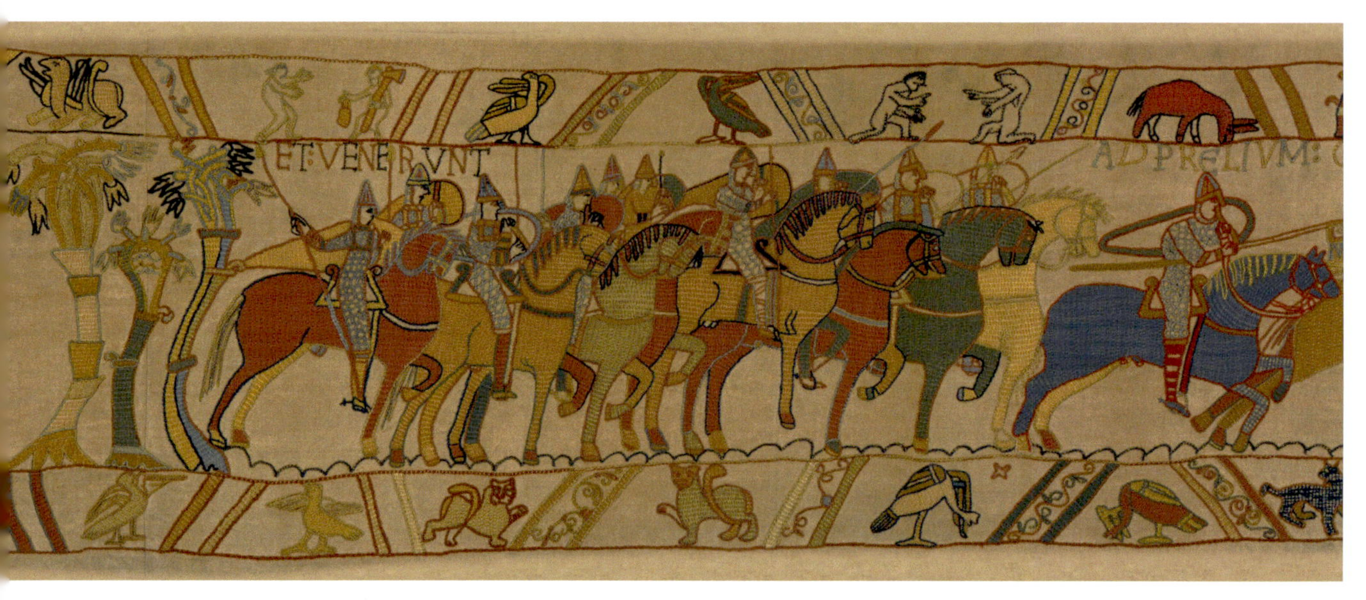

William's Norman cavalry then gallops off to face Harold's English soldiers.

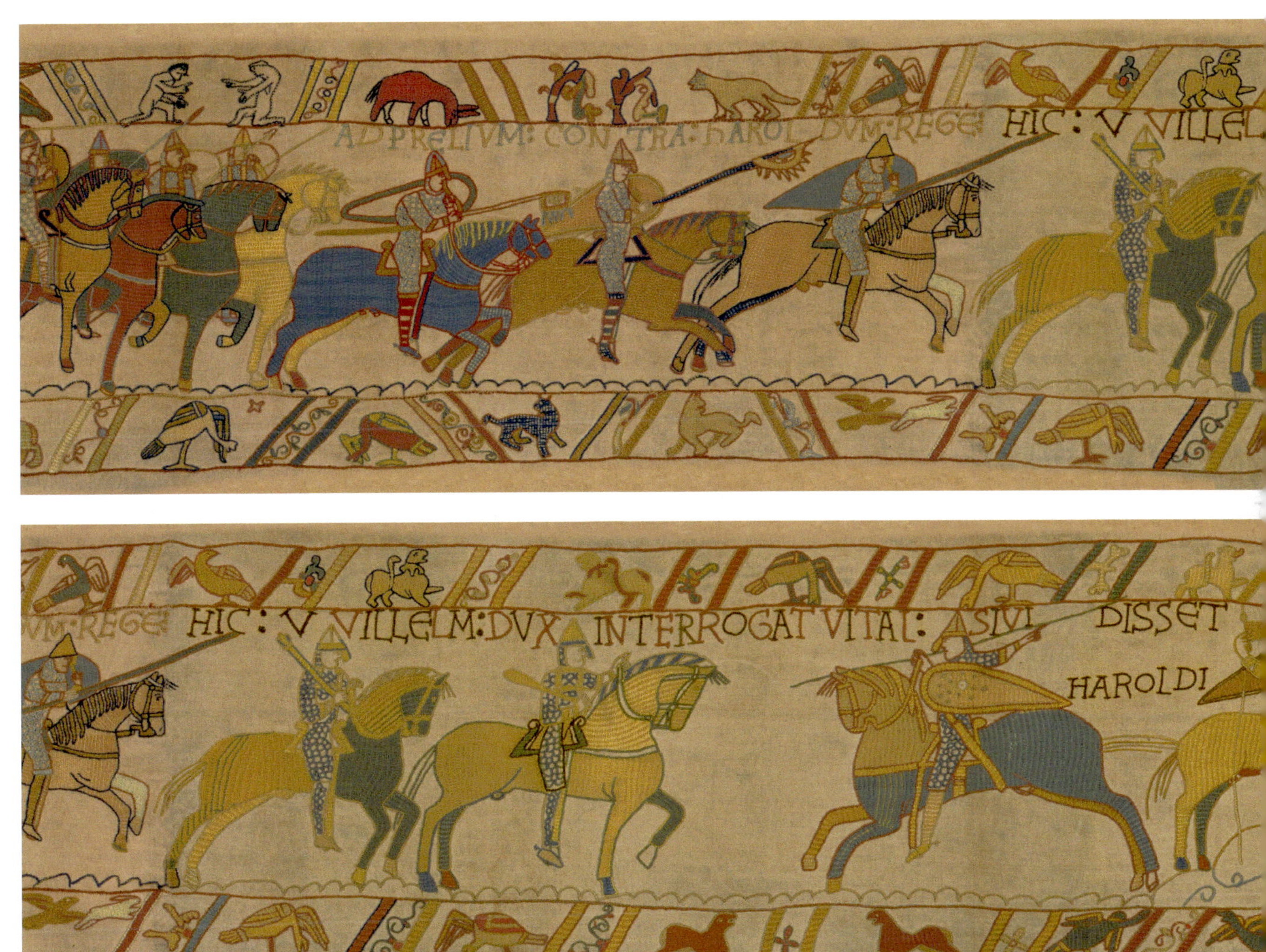

William is shown twice: first leading a trio of mounted soldiers at the head of his troops, then immediately to the right (on a different-coloured horse!) asking Vital (one of Odo's followers) if the enemy has been seen yet.

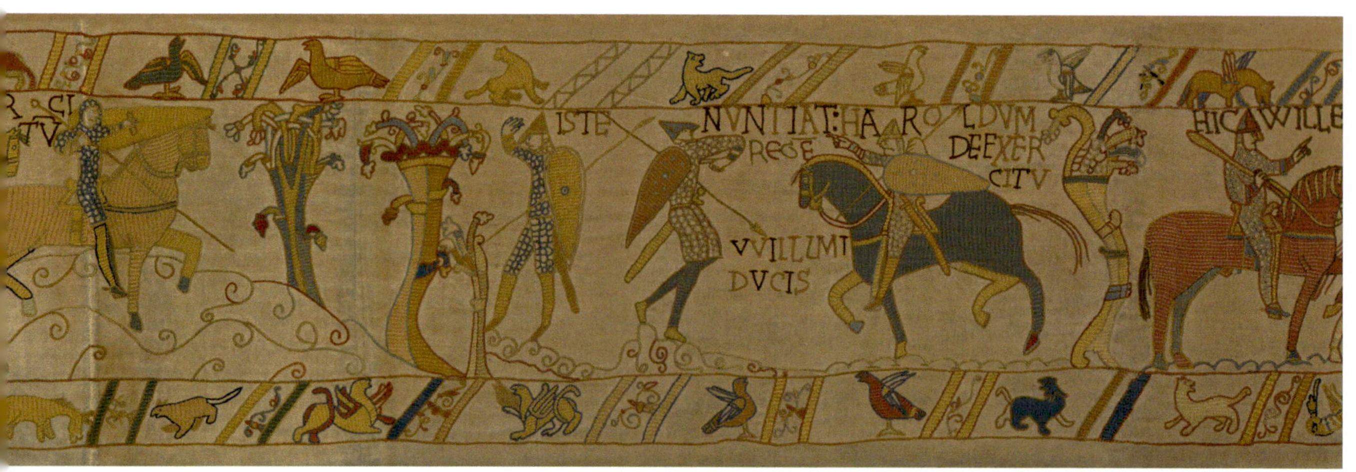

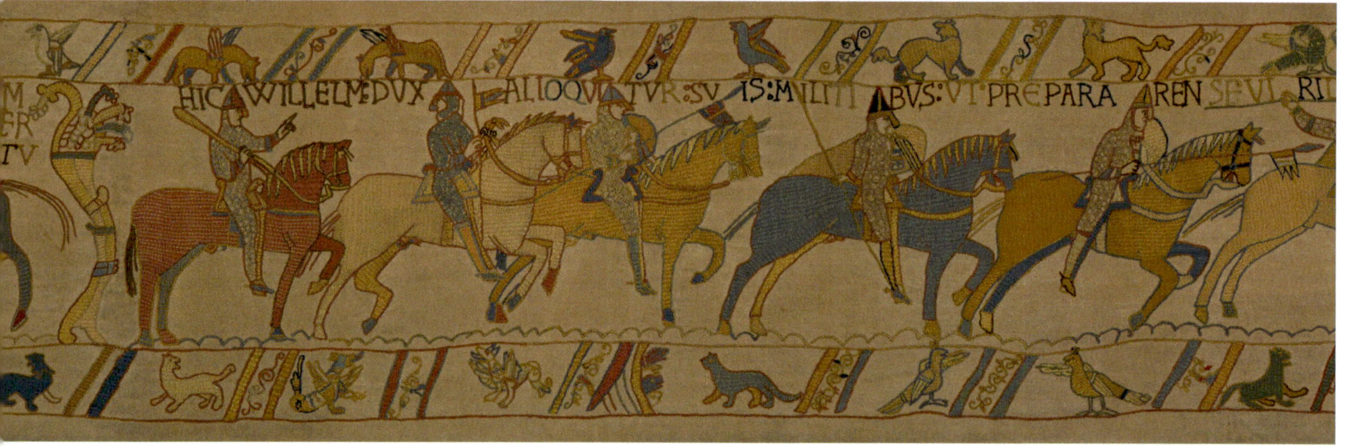

The scene changes to the English side. A look-out, to the right of the trees, warns Harold that the Norman army is approaching.

Back on the Norman side, William, mace in hand, gives a speech to encourage his soldiers.

The clerics in the tapestry

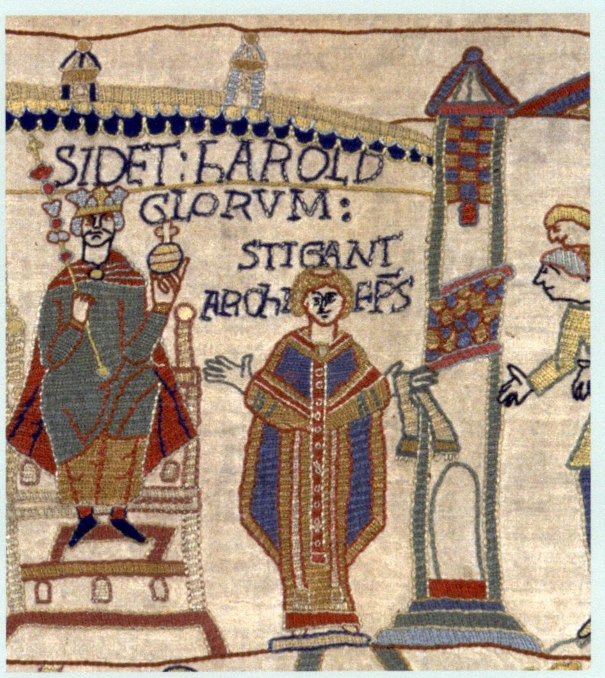

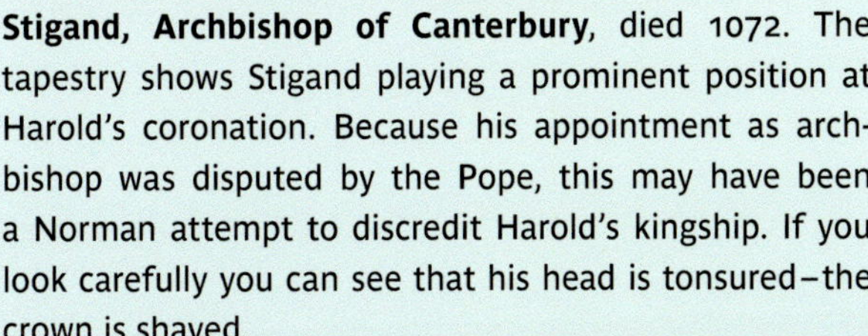

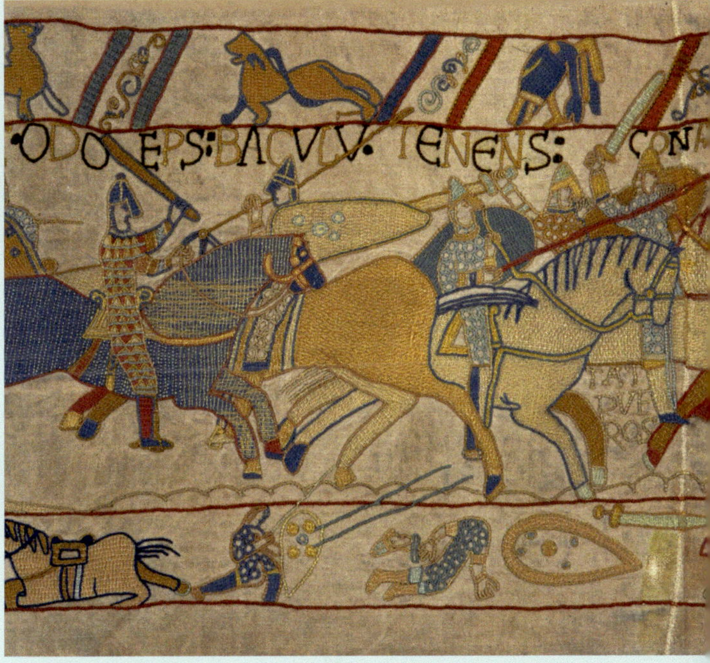

Stigand, Archbishop of Canterbury, died 1072. The tapestry shows Stigand playing a prominent position at Harold's coronation. Because his appointment as archbishop was disputed by the Pope, this may have been a Norman attempt to discredit Harold's kingship. If you look carefully you can see that his head is tonsured – the crown is shaved.

Odo, Bishop of Bayeux, died 1097. Half-brother of William I, Odo is thought to have commissioned the original tapestry, possibly during the 15-year period from 1067 when William left him in charge of England as Earl of Kent, while he returned to Normandy. Odo's name appears several times and, although a churchman, he is shown taking part in the battle at Hastings.

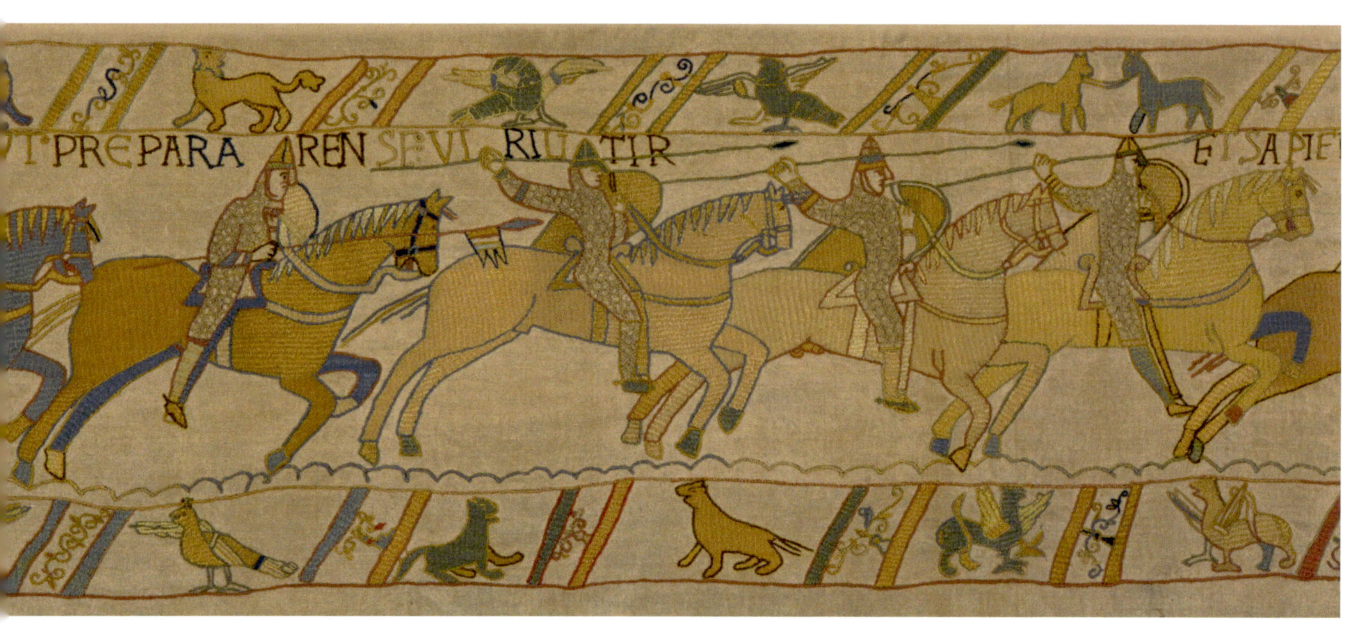

The Normans charge …

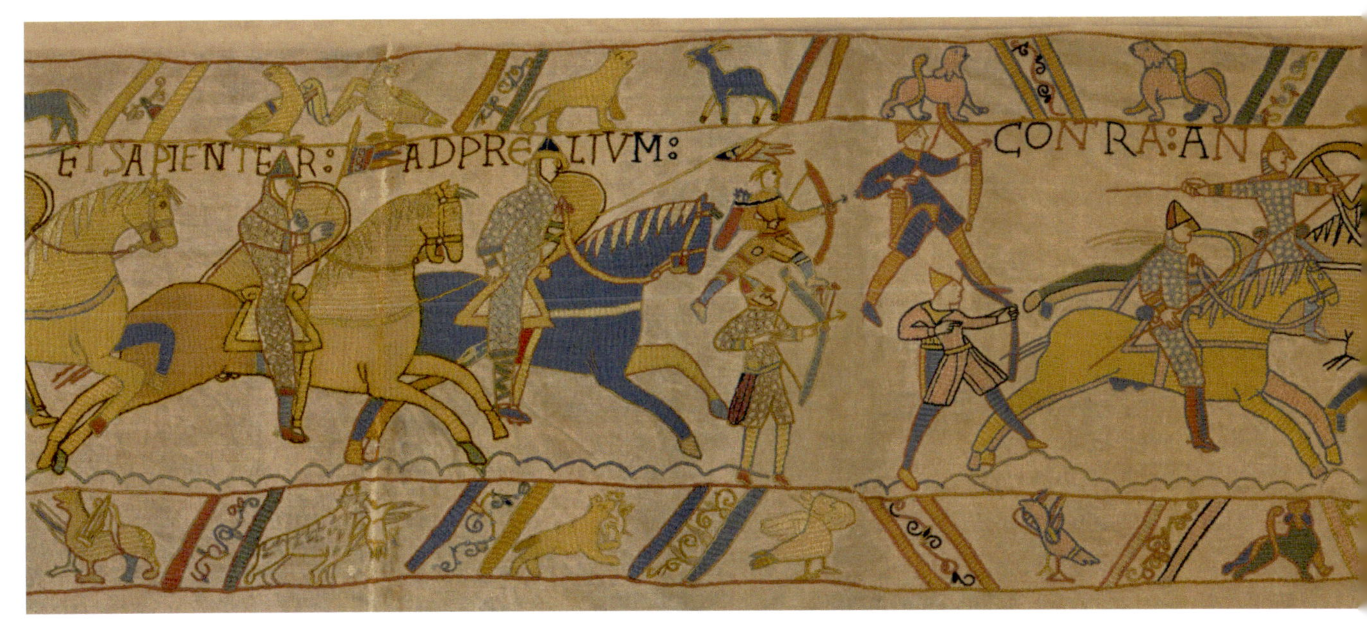

... and the Battle of Hastings has begun.

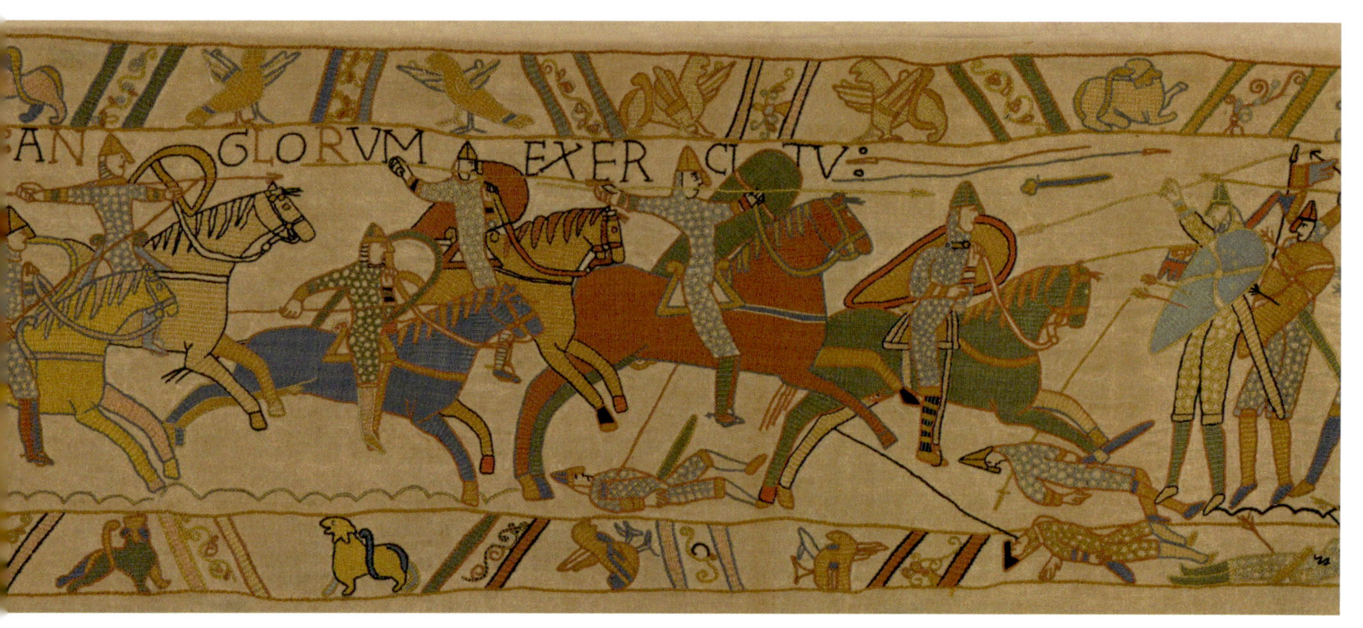

As the air fills with arrows and lances, men lie dying.

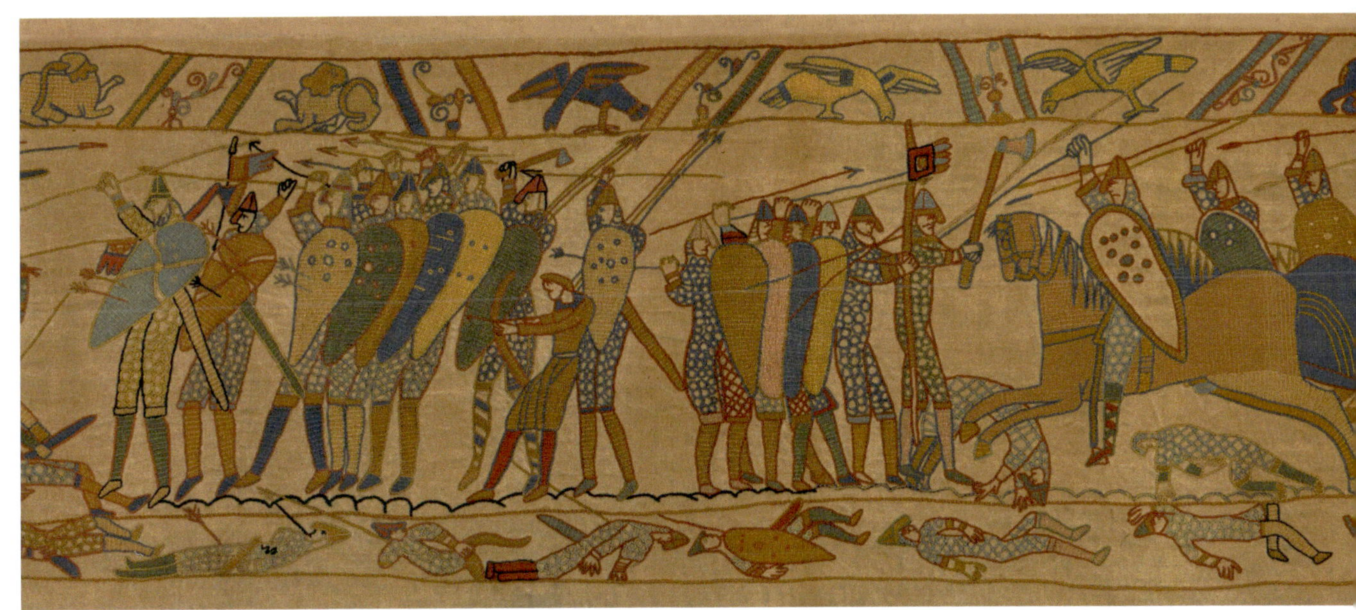

The English soldiers, who are all on foot, protect themselves with a wall of shields. The lower border of the tapestry is filled with dead and injured soldiers.

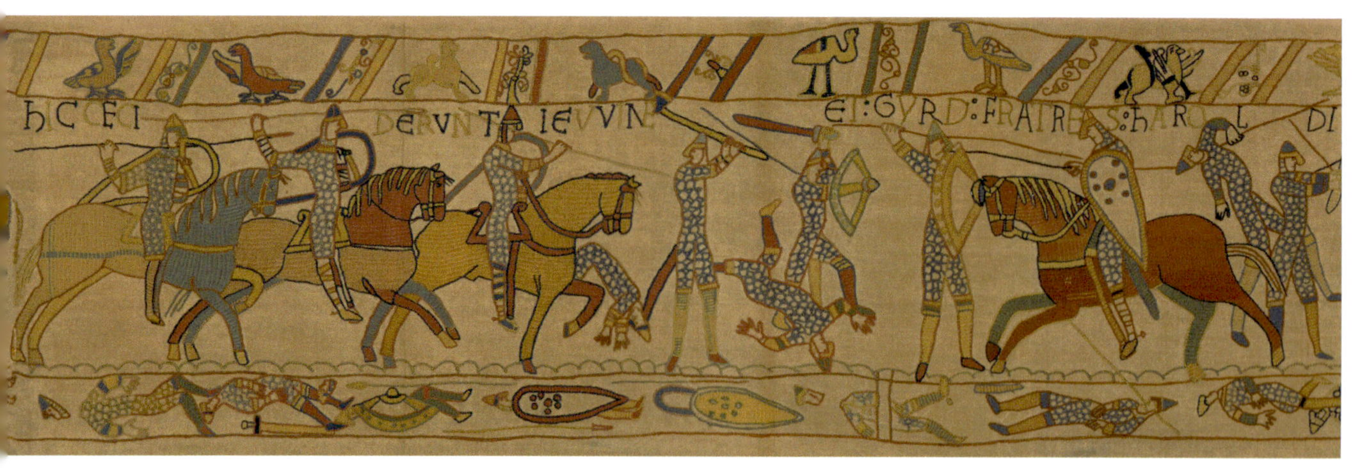

The violence continues as men hack and spear each other to death. Harold's brothers, Lewine and Gyrd, both die fighting.

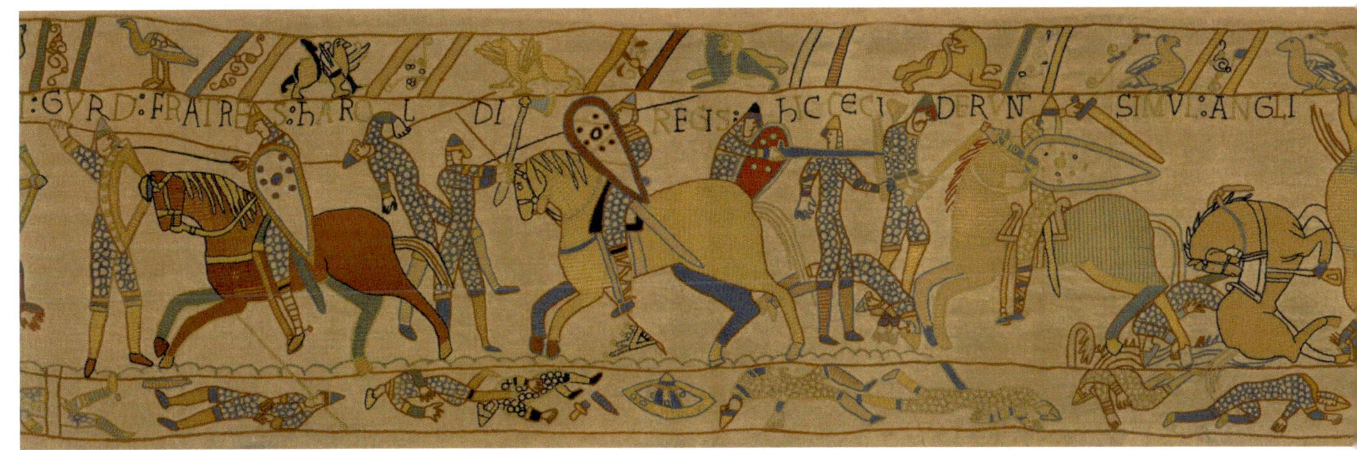

The battle rages on; men and horses crash to the ground; the lower border is strewn with slaughtered troops and animals.

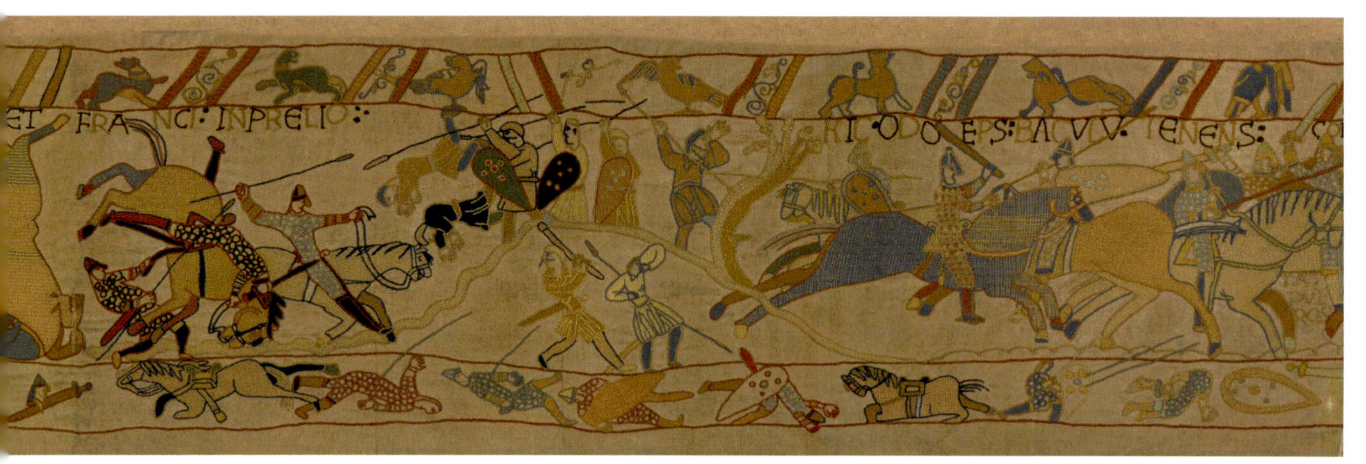

Bishop Odo appears in the thick of the fighting, waving a club and encouraging his followers. Odo uses a club rather than a sword as bishops were not supposed to shed blood.

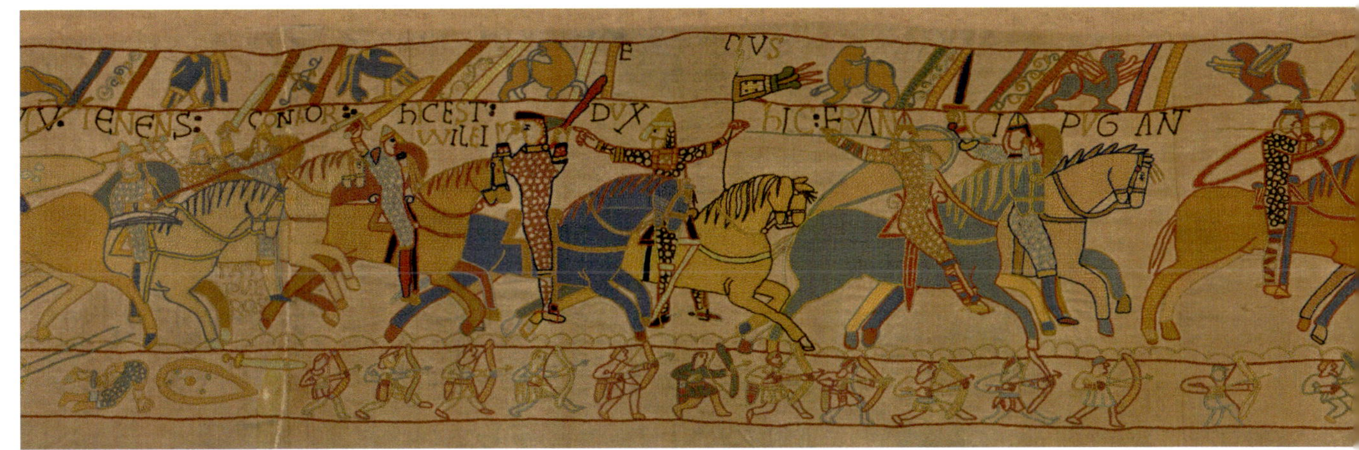

After a fall from his horse, William raises his helmet to reveal his face. This shows his troops that he is still alive and encourages them to continue fighting. Count Eustace carries an elaborate banner, which may be the one given by the Pope to show his support for William's invasion of England.

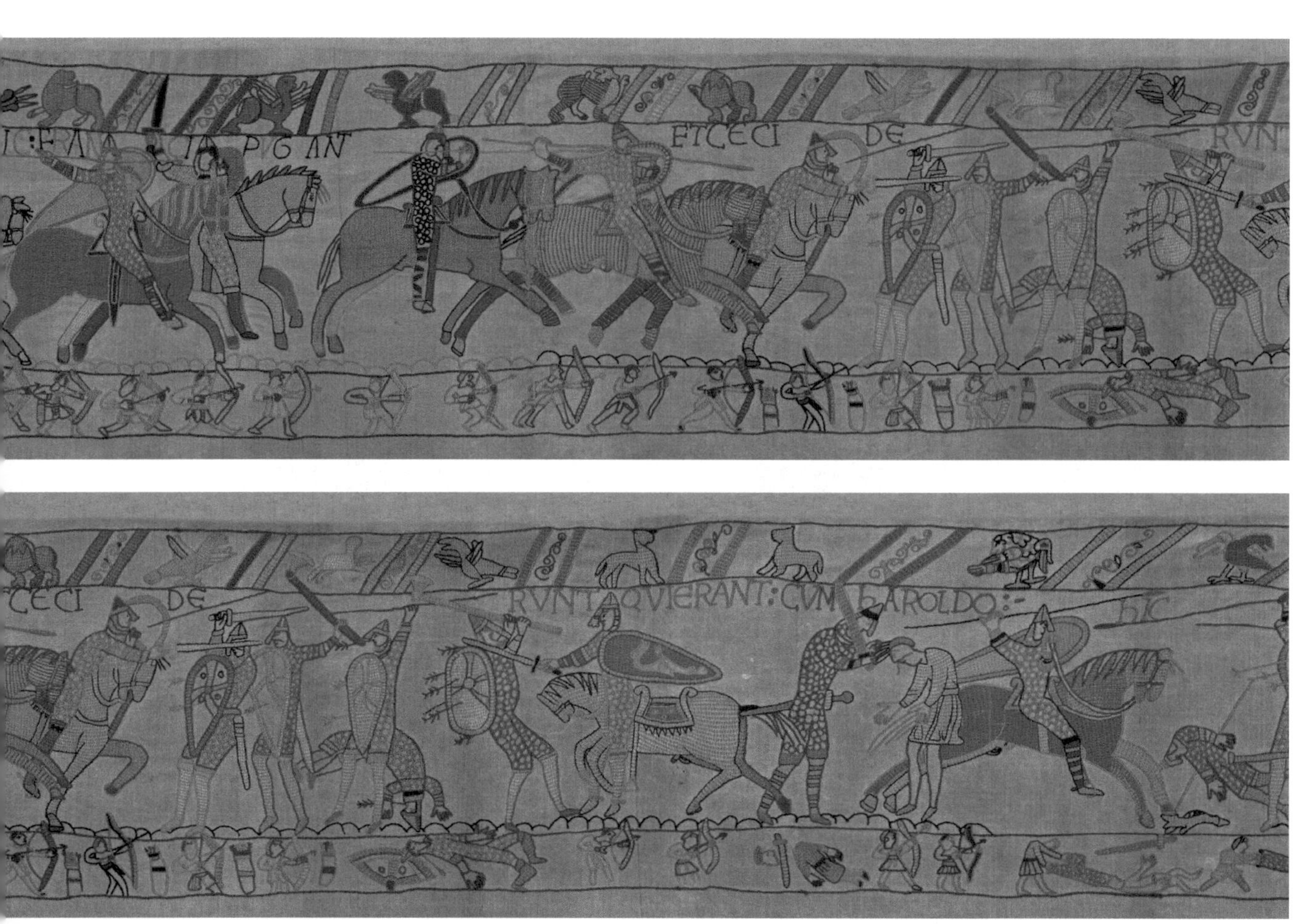

The Normans seem to be getting the upper hand as the battle continues.

Many more soldiers die, one appears to be having his head cut off.

The women in the tapestry

Only three women are shown in the main narrative of the tapestry.

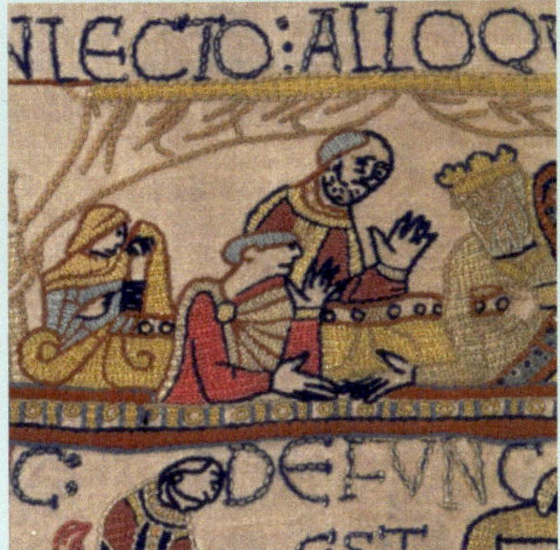

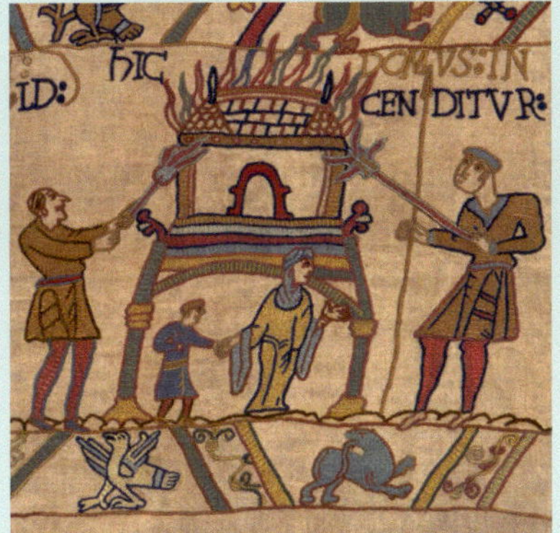

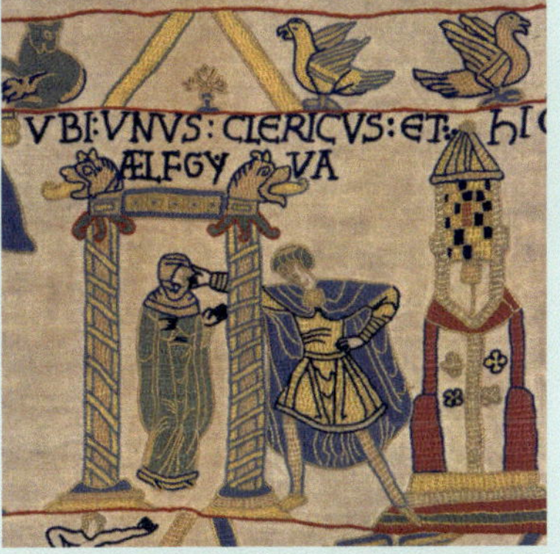

Edith. This figure must be Edith, wife of Edward the Confessor and sister of King Harold. The author of the *Life of Edward*, written soon after his death, records that she was present at Edward's death-bed when he commended her to Harold's protection.

This woman is shown either trapped inside or fleeing from a burning building at Hastings when William's troops were harrying the area.

Aelfgyva. The meaning of this scene is obscure. However, it must refer to a well-known event to be in such a prominent position. Aelfgyva was a widely used Saxon name.

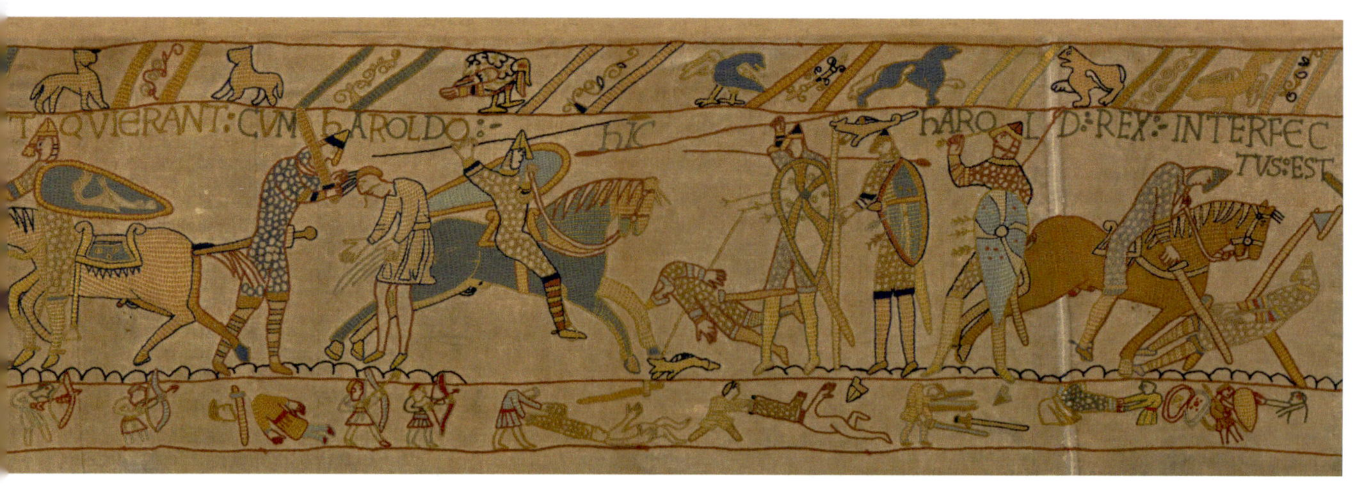

The best-known scene in the tapestry: the Normans killing King Harold. But how is Harold killed? He seems to be shown twice: first plucking an arrow from his eye, and then being struck on his thigh by the heavy sword of a French knight. The tapestry is difficult to interpret here, but the second figure is probably Harold being killed.

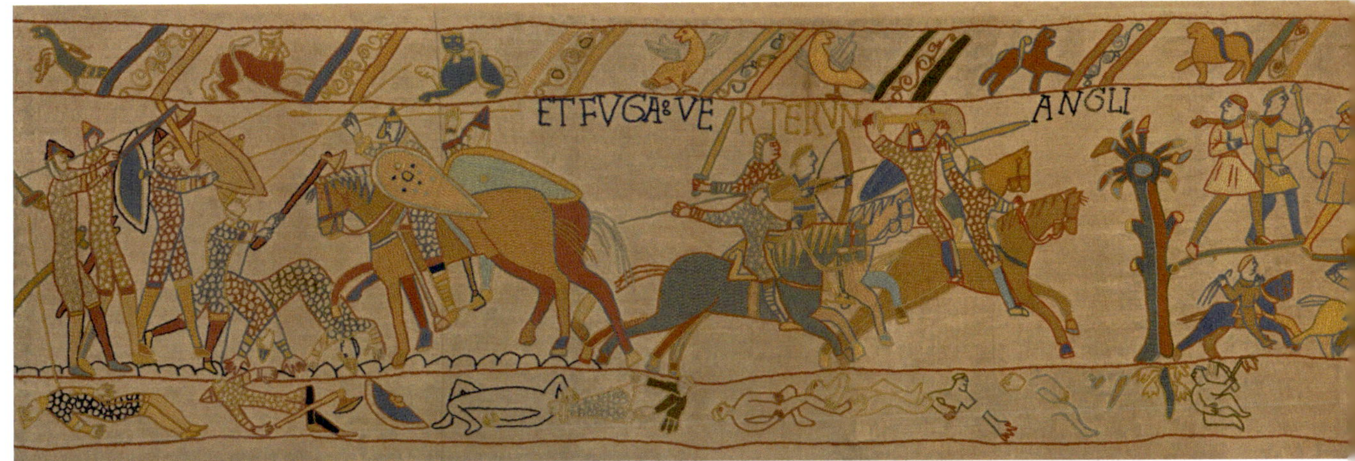

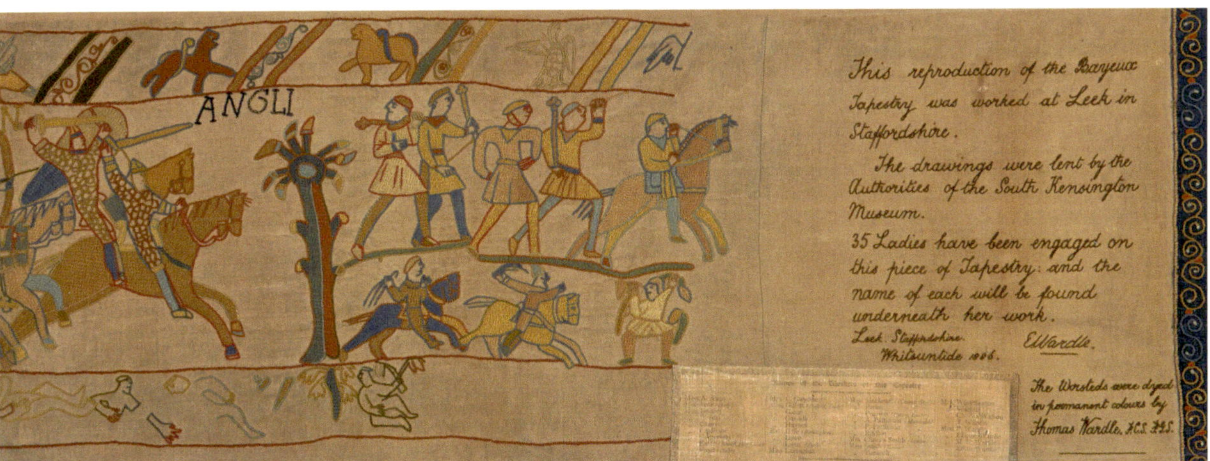

This reproduction of the Bayeux Tapestry was worked at Leek in Staffordshire.

The drawings were lent by the Authorities of the South Kensington Museum.

35 Ladies have been engaged on this piece of Tapestry: and the name of each will be found underneath her work.

Leek. Staffordshire. Whitsuntide 1886.

ElWardle.

The Worsteds were dyed in permanent colours by Thomas Wardle, F.C.S. F.G.S.

14 October 1066. With Harold dead, the battle continues for a short while. But soon the victorious Normans chase the remaining English from the battle-field. The final scene from the tapestry has been lost. It may have shown William being crowned king of England. This would match the scene at the very beginning of the tapestry that shows King Edward, secure on the throne just two years earlier.

What happened next?

After the Battle of Hastings, William still had to conquer England. He marched from Hastings, crossing the Thames at Wallingford, and then on towards London. At Berkhamsted he received the surrender of the city. William took hostages to ensure that the surrender was kept.

William wanted to be crowned king as soon as possible. His coronation took place on Christmas Day, 1066. It was held at Westminster Abbey, which had been built by Edward the Confessor, and where Harold had been crowned earlier that year. During the coronation, as the people inside the abbey shouted out their acceptance of William, the troops outside thought a fight had broken out. Fearing that William had been attacked, they began to set fire to Saxon houses. As the Norman soldiers could not understand the language of the Saxons, and the Saxons could not understand the language of the Normans, it was difficult for them to communicate. So began the reign of the Norman kings of England.

The Norman Conquest had a direct impact on Reading. In 1100 William's youngest son Henry became king of England and in 1121 founded Reading Abbey. This new religious community became one of Europe's most important medieval monasteries and its large Romanesque church was Henry's burial place, dominating the town until the monastery's dissolution in 1539.

The ruins of Reading Abbey, post-restoration, in 2018.

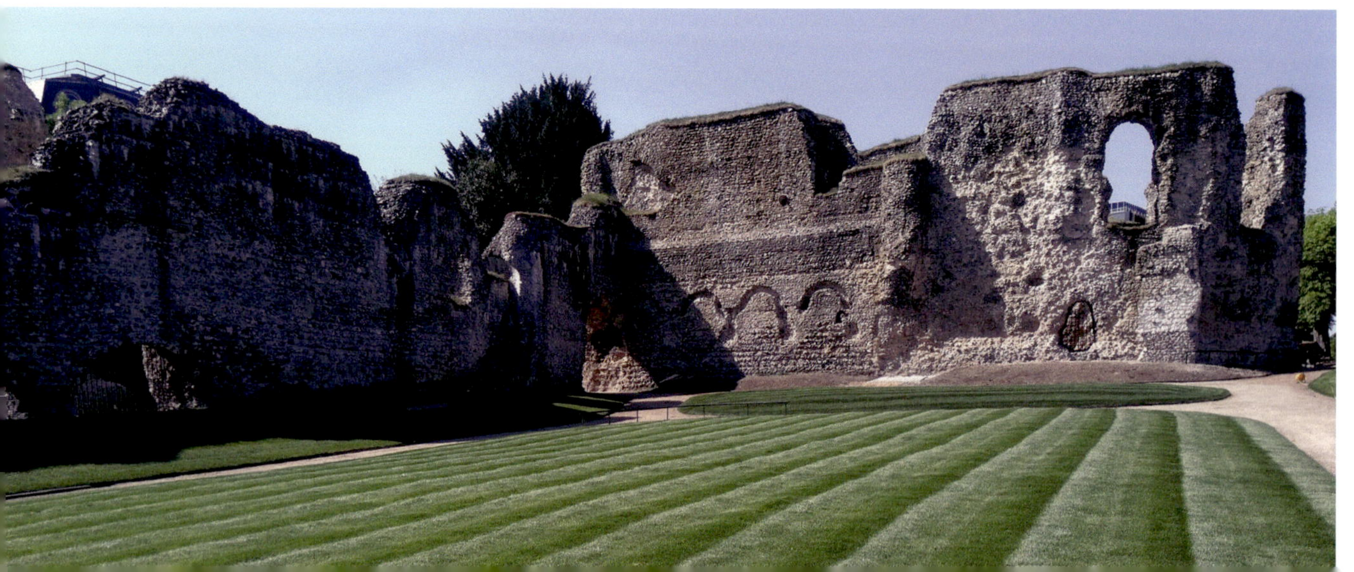

Bibliography

Bayeux Museum, *La Tapisserie De Bayeux: Reproduction intégrale au 1/7.*

Andrew Bridgeford, *1066: The Hidden History in the Bayeux Tapestry*, Harper Perennial, 2011

Rev. J.C. Bruce, *The Bayeux Tapestry Elucidated*, 1856

Carola Hicks, *Bayeux Tapestry: The life story of a masterpiece*, London 2006

Anne Jacques, *Leek Embroidery*, Staffordshire County Council, 1990

Anne Jacques, *The Wardle Story*, Churnet Valley Books (pages 61–66 on the tapestry), 1996

Eric Maclagan, *The Bayeux Tapestry,* King Penguin Books, 1943

Reading Standard, 20 February, 1909

Frank M. Stenton, ed. *The Bayeux Tapestry: A Comprehensive Survey.* Phaidon Press, 1957

Dennis Stuart, ed. *The History of the Leek Embroidery Society*, Keele University Department of Adult Education, 1969

Charlie Rozier, 'Stitches in Time: A History of the Bayeux Tapestry', *History Today*, 2018

Mrs T. Wardle, *Guide to the Bayeux Tapestry*, London 1887

Christine Woods, 'Sir Thomas Wardle', entry in the *Dictionary of Business Biography* Vol 5, Butterworth, 1986

Two Rivers Press has been publishing in and about Reading since 1994.
Founded by the artist Peter Hay (1951–2003), the press continues
to delight readers, local and further afield, with its varied list
of individually designed, thought-provoking books.

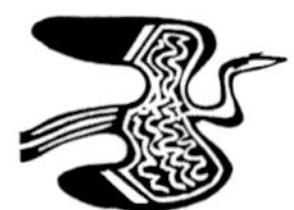

This book is set in Parisine, a contemporary, reassuringly regular sanserif
originally designed as a signage typeface for the Paris Métro. Described by
its designer, Jean François Porchez, as 'human, but not fancy', we thought
its nature and its French pedigree were appropriate for this story.